Archers, Alchemists,
and 98 Other Medieval Jobs You Might Have Loved or Loathed

by Priscilla Galloway
art by Martha Newbigging

Annick Press Ltd.
Toronto • New York • Vancouver

We acknowledge the support of the Canada Council
for the Arts, the Ontario Arts Council, the Government
of Ontario through the Ontario Book Publishers Tax
Credit program and the Ontario Book Initiative, and
the Government of Canada through the Book
Publishing Industry Development Program (BPIDP) for
our publishing activities.

Cataloging in Publication

Galloway, Priscilla, 1930-
   Archers, alchemists, and 98 other medieval jobs
you might have loved or loathed / by Priscilla Galloway ;
art by Martha Newbigging.

Includes index.
ISBN 1-55037-811-2 (bound).
ISBN 1-55037-810-4 (pbk.)

   1. Civilization, Medieval—Juvenile literature.
2. Occupations—History—To 1500—Juvenile literature.
I. Newbigging, Martha II. Title. III. Title: Archers,
Alchemists, and ninety-eight other medieval jobs you
might have loved or loathed.

CB351.G34 2003   j909.07
C2003-901862-8

Distributed in Canada by:
Firefly Books Ltd.
66 Leek Avenue
Richmond Hill, ON
L4B 1H1

Published in the U.S.A. by Annick Press (U.S.) Ltd.
Distributed in the U.S.A. by:
Firefly Books (U.S.) Inc
P.O. Box 1338
Ellicott Station
Buffalo, NY 14205

Printed and bound in Belgium.

Visit us at: www.annickpress.com

To my chief educational consultants, my daughter Noël and her spouse Wayne, with love. —P.G.

To my true blue, Almerinda—M.N.

Contents

Introduction

This book is about some of the jobs you might do if you went back to live in Europe in the Middle Ages.

You probably already know a few things about the Middle Ages, about knights and castles, Robin Hood and Maid Marian, good King Richard and bad King John. Films, TV, and stories show those times as full of thrilling adventures. Sherwood Forest seems like the best kind of summer camp, with archery and horseback riding and dinner around the campfire, and nobody making you mind your manners. It seldom rains in Sherwood, and never snows. The outlaws are the good guys, and they always defeat the wicked sheriff and his men.

But films and TV, even when the makers do their best to get it right, don't tell you much about how people really lived. And they cover only a short period of time. The Middle Ages went on for about a thousand years, from 450 to 1450–1500 CE. That's 10 times 100 years—or 100 times 10 years. (How long have you been alive?) A thousand years is a long, long time. If you divide that thousand years in half, this book is about jobs in Europe in the second half, from 1000 to 1500 CE.

There's plenty this book does *not* tell you about the Middle Ages. This is lucky, because a book that big would be too long to read. You'd have to take out a bank loan to buy it and hire a truck to drive it home. Instead, this book will give you a chance to explore 100 different jobs you might have loved or hated all those centuries ago.

What happened when?

The Roman Empire was kaput, finished, done. Vandals burned the ancient city of Rome, and Europe sank into the first half of the Middle Ages, the Dark Ages. Why "dark"? Partly because a lot of things people knew in earlier times were lost or forgotten. Libraries and other records were destroyed; learned people couldn't get jobs so they did other things and learning disappeared. In the succeeding centuries, kings ruled, Vikings invaded, people lived and died. There wasn't one big country anymore, but a lot of little ones that kept changing.

Lifetime of Muhammad, founder of Islam, born in Mecca.

About 450 CE   **570–632**

711 CE

Moorish conquest of Spain (led by caliphs from Arab lands). Arab countries had preserved records from ancient Egypt, Greece, and Rome. Muslim scholars used the old knowledge and built on it. The resulting Islamic culture influenced the rest of Europe from this base in Spain as well as, later, through the crusades. During the next 700 years, however, Christians gradually reconquered Spain—in time for Queen Isabella to give ships and money to Christopher Columbus in 1492.

Now, fast forward out of the Dark Ages to...

Norman Conquest. Duke William of Normandy (now part of France) beat King Harold of England when one of William's archers landed an arrow in Harold's eye. French became the high-class language in England. English was now low-class.

King John of England was forced to sign *Magna Carta*, the "Great Charter." The barons wanted to make sure the king couldn't slap taxes on them whenever he wanted, or make up excuses to behead them and seize their lands. The barons were looking after themselves, but they looked after us at the same time, because many rights that you have today started with *Magna Carta* in 1215: "No freeman shall be taken and imprisoned or disseised [dispossessed] or exiled or in any way destroyed . . . except by the lawful judgment of his peers and by the law of the land."

1066

1096

1215

First Crusade. Other crusades followed for almost 200 years. These were religious wars. Muslims ruled Jerusalem, and European Christians wanted it. This was holy land for both religions, and they kept fighting over it.

Downside: Many people were killed and wounded; poverty and high taxes resulted because kings and countries spent too much on war.

Upside: European crusaders took new knowledge home, and doctors, mathematicians, and architects in Europe used it in new ways.

Little Ice Age. Colder weather, shorter growing seasons; millions of hungry people. The colder weather lasted longer than the end of the Middle Ages.

1300–1700

1348–1350

1492

The Plague, also called the Black Death; millions of dead people and dead rats; billions of dead fleas. There weren't enough peasants in Europe to farm all the land. This meant better lives for the peasants who were left, since the landowners needed them.

Columbus sailed to America. End of the Middle Ages.

Of course, it wasn't really so neat. The Middle Ages didn't end all at once, but 1492 is a handy date to remember.

Many other things happened in the thousand years of the Middle Ages. You can fit them into the big picture when you learn about them.

How many people lived there?

We don't know exactly how many people lived in Europe in the Middle Ages, but there weren't nearly as many as today. Populations grew twice, three times, or even four times as big between 1000 and 1300 CE. In the next 200 years, however, 1300 to 1500, the number of people living in Europe hardly changed at all. Why? (Hint: Look at the timeline to see what happened in 1348–50.)

A thousand years ago, the same number of people lived in the British Isles as live today in Vancouver or Houston. Five hundred years ago, the whole population of Britain was only a little bigger than that of present-day Toronto or Los Angeles. Today, more people live in New York and Tokyo than in the whole of Europe a thousand years ago. In 1300, about 35,000 people lived in London; London is 200 times bigger today.

By our standards, even the biggest places in the Middle Ages were small. Your classroom has more people in it than some villages did then. You can see there would be more open space, more forests and wild lands in those days. Most people lived in the country. Only one out of every 20 people lived in cities and towns.

How was life different then?

Your life in the Middle Ages would have been very different from your life today. The smells would have turned your stomach; you'd have to survive without orange juice, cereal, soft drinks, or fast food; and you would long in vain for a flush toilet, a shower, or a shampoo.

But the biggest difference between life today and life in the Middle Ages wasn't something you could grasp with your senses. If you could go back to live in those times, even if your language and clothes were right, even if you were ready for the food, smells, and sanitation, even if you knew everything you needed for the job you'd chosen, you would keep saying and doing things wrong, because of one basic difference between now and then.

The way we think today, you are important; so is everyone else. In the Canadian Charter of Rights and Freedoms, in the Constitution of the United States, individual rights and freedoms come first. In the United Kingdom, *Magna Carta* laid the foundation for similar rights and freedoms, and British common law has extended them over the centuries. One person has the same rights and freedoms as another. Our social organization and laws are mostly based on this belief. Even the worst criminals have rights.

In the Middle Ages, the underlying belief was the other way around. The whole structure was far more important than any individual. From king to peasant, you had your place in the world. Your rights and freedoms depended on your place, and your place depended on birth, not on ability. Compared to our world, your rights and freedoms were very limited, even if you were a king. People in those days probably didn't live up to their beliefs any better than we do today, but you could not expect to win an argument based on an idea of your own rights. The student had no right to disagree with the teacher, or the apprentice with the master—or the child with his or her parents, even if the child was right and the adults were wrong. Rebellion brought swift punishment.

Everybody in their place

In the Middle Ages, Christians believed that God put people where they belonged, so you should not try to change your place in society. Of course, some people did try. If you succeeded, that was part of God's plan; if you failed, you were punished, sometimes cruelly.

Keeping everybody in place involved a chain of command—the feudal system. Everybody owed "homage and fealty" to somebody above: the peasant to the lord of the manor (maybe a knight), the knight to his lord (maybe a baron), the baron or baroness to their lord (maybe a king), and the king to God, who was Lord of all. When you made your oath of homage and fealty, you entered into an agreement with your lord; by accepting it, he made an agreement with you. The details of these agreements varied widely, but in one way or another you promised to be faithful to your lord and to provide certain services, usually including military service, though a woman might give money instead. Your lord promised to respect his agreement with you, including your rights as his vassal over land or estates he might have granted.

There were four main groups of people in the Middle Ages. People in every group had their duties.

NOBLES

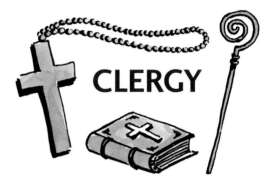

CLERGY

The clergy and other Church people had their work: to care for human souls. Christians in the Middle Ages believed that you would be punished forever if you did wrong and did not repent and receive forgiveness before you died. There were lots of other rules about what you could and could not do; Church courts dispensed justice too.

If you were born to noble parents, you were noble. If you were born a peasant, you were a peasant. A noble could not be a peasant, and a peasant could not be a noble, and that was that. Some members of the clergy were noble; others were not. Within the Church, however, if you were smart and lucky, you might gain power and recognition and be treated like a noble even if you weren't one.

The nobility had their work: to govern others and dispense justice, providing an orderly and safe life on their lands; to look like nobles and live like nobles; to go to war when called by their lords, with whatever support they had sworn to bring, such as a specific number of knights and other fighting men with arms and armor according to their rank.

SPECIALISTS

PEASANTS

*I*n castles, abbeys, and towns, some people developed special skills, such as armorer, illuminator, baker, goldsmith, or furrier. Some specialized in medicine or law; still others became manufacturers and merchants. These people also found their places in the

orderly world. Many of them owned or worked for businesses in towns. Their ideals were honesty and excellence, not high profits. However, some of them did become rich and powerful. Although they were not noble, they and their families sometimes lived better than many of the poorer nobility.

*P*easants were at the bottom of the social scale. They had their work: to farm the land, producing food for everybody; to work or fight for their lord; to pay fees and taxes to their lord, and a tithe to the Church. With all this work to do—and no time for play—a peasant's life was very hard.

People didn't always live up to the ideal. Some nobles spent their time and money looking like nobles and living like nobles without protecting their people. A noble lord's idea of justice might be to hang anybody who disagreed with him. Clergy did not always care for human souls. Merchants sometimes charged high prices for shoddy goods. Peasants could not always grow enough food, and they were usually the ones who went hungry.

Oath of homage and fealty

What follows is part of a very long oath of homage and fealty made in 1110 CE by Viscount Bernard Atton of Carcassonne to his liege lord Leo, abbot of the monastery of St. Mary of Grasse. Viscount Bernard was the abbot's vassal. Bernard held power over about 20 properties granted by the abbot. In turn, lesser knights would have held property from Viscount Bernard and sworn oaths to him, and they would be his vassals.

In his oath, Bernard promises his lord he will always be faithful. He will defend the abbot and the monks of St. Mary of Grasse and all their possessions. The viscount will also give back everything the abbot has granted to him any time the abbot says so. Then comes the part about holding the horse's stirrup when the abbot mounts. Nobles in the Middle Ages were proud. Viscount Bernard would never have done a groom's job for anyone else; however, there was no dishonor in doing the humblest personal service for your lord.

While making this oath, Bernard would kneel and place his hands in the abbot's hands.

I make homage and fealty with hands and with mouth to thee my said lord abbot Leo and to thy successors, and I swear … that I will always be a faithful vassal to thee and to thy successors and to St. Mary of Grasse … and I will defend thee, my lord, and all thy successors, and the said monastery and the monks present and to come and the castles and manors and all your men and their possessions against all male- factors and invaders … and I will give to thee power over all the castles and manors above described … whenever they shall be claimed by thee or by thy successors …

And when the abbot shall mount his horse I and my heirs, viscounts of Carcassonne, and our successors ought to hold the stirrup for the honor of the dominion of St. Mary of Grasse …

Women in the Middle Ages

The Middle Ages was a good period for women in Europe, though not nearly as good as today. However, medieval women could run a business, rule an abbey, defend a castle, teach at a university, practise medicine, learn a skilled trade, earn a living by writing, and own land and houses with the power to buy and sell.

This is not to say that women everywhere in Europe did all these things, or that women in general had the same rights and powers as men. They didn't. Women, like men, were part of the structured society, with everybody in his or her place, and a wife's place was subordinate to her husband. In England, a husband had the legal right to beat his wife with a rod, as long as the rod was no thicker than his thumb.

However, in the centuries after the Middle Ages, things got better for men and worse for women. Until very recent times, men continued to gain rights and powers, while women lost them. Less than 100 years ago, men could vote, but women could not; women could not attend university along with men. History books ignored women. But now we recognize everyone's importance in history. Both women and men among your ancestors helped to give you the opportunities you have today.

Never an idle moment

In the Middle Ages, there were no factories and very few machines. From nails and needles to castles and cathedrals, everything was made by hand, one at a time. You might go hungry; you might live in a hut; you might be dressed in rags—but if you were able and willing, you would have work.

What kind of work?

That depended on which group you belonged to (nobles, clergy, specialists, or peasants), and whether you were a boy or a girl, although gender did not always make a difference. Children usually did the same work as their fathers and mothers.

People in the Middle Ages did not have childhoods as people do today; they grew up quickly. A young person's duty was to obey and help his or her parents. Even the hours in your day belonged to someone else, not to you. You began to take your place in the world of work almost as soon as you could toddle. A peasant child of three might keep his baby sister from falling into the cooking fire; a five- or six-year-old could work in the fields. Noble children were often sent to be breast-fed by a peasant mother with a baby of her own, a good job for the mother but a huge responsibility at a time when many babies died. If the foster children lived through the first year or two, they went home to begin their training as nobles.

In the Middle Ages, a boy couldn't expect to grow up with his family. If his family was noble, his parents would usually send him to another noble family when he was about seven years old, to serve as a page. Boys from non-noble families were often sent away as well. If a boy was going to learn a craft or trade, he would become an apprentice. Somebody, usually his father, made a written agreement with the boy's master and paid a fee for the training. The boy could not leave his master's service for the term of the contract, which could last as long as seven or even ten years. He lived in his master's household, and was supposed to be treated like a child of the family, but frequently became more like a servant or even a slave.

When did children in the Middle Ages learn their reading, writing, and arithmetic? Didn't they go to school? No, they didn't, and they really didn't need to. Most boys and girls in the Middle Ages never learned to read, write, or calculate beyond what they picked up in their training or on the job. Today, in the Information Age, literacy and computer skills are vital, just as skill with a knight's lance, a peasant's hoe, or a weaver's loom were vital then.

Medieval girls sometimes lived apart from their families too. A girl might become a servant in a noble or rich household, although she might stay at home until she married, perhaps in her mid- or late teens. A girl in a noble family would be closely supervised. She might be taught at home, or might go as a lady-in-waiting to another noble family. A noble girl might marry even earlier than a girl from a poor family, since her marriage was usually a kind of merger of lands, titles, and wealth, and the sooner the merger took place, the better. Peasants might marry because they cared for each other; nobles might never meet before their wedding day.

Choosing a Medieval career

Little time of your own, little private space, not much family life, and almost no individual rights: you can easily see how difficult it would be for you to go along with all of that. Today, we expect to choose the kind of work we do: police officer, mail carrier, firefighter, actor, journalist, teacher, accountant, plumber, aerospace scientist, banker, veterinarian, ice skater, marine biologist, to name only a few possibilities.

It wasn't like that in the Middle Ages, but let's pretend you could try out any of the jobs in this book. It's fun to choose—so use this guide to find careers you might have loved or loathed. Be a great noble, then a gong farmer (latrine cleaner), a doctor or a village healer, an abbess or a goldsmith. Try jobs heartwarming and heavenly, or dirty and desperate.

Turn the page!

CHAPTER ONE
Bread and Butter Jobs

Today, we buy many of the things we need, and they come to us from all over the world. In Europe in the Middle Ages, most items for ordinary people were made and used locally. Your daily needs depended on the kind of life you led. In summer, peasants worked in bare feet or with rags tied on; in winter, they wore rough wooden clogs, often carved by someone in the family. However, even poor country folk must have felt they needed better footwear: there were more cobblers than any other kind of skilled worker, one for every 150 people. That's like one cobbler to make and mend shoes just for the people in five classes at your school. On the other hand, there was only one blacksmith for every 1,500 people—one blacksmith to shoe horses and do ironwork for as many people as you'd find in three or four schools put together. Ordinary people didn't own much, and they mended everything.

There are two things that everybody needs: food and drink. The first seven jobs in this chapter tell about people who grew and processed these everyday items. Everybody needs clothes, too; five jobs tell about people who made cloth or shoes. The cloth trade was very important in the Middle Ages, the way making cars is important today. In most towns, there were different careers for different parts of this

work, such as weaver, spinster, furrier, fuller, merchant tailor, dyer, arras-maker (maker of tapestry wall-hangings), embroiderer, lacemaker, and bonnet-maker.

Most people lived in the country, however, not in towns, and they didn't move around much. They made everything possible themselves, and they traded with their neighbors. Most country people could do many jobs, though usually not well, since they didn't have training or practice or good tools. Peddlers traveled from place to place with things that people might pay for, such as needles and pots and pans, even though pots were mended until they wore out, and a poor family might own only one needle, one pot, and one or two knives.

Some jobs in this chapter were located in the country, some in the towns, and some could be in either. Merchants generally lived in towns, though some of them took goods around to country fairs. Those doing these jobs were ordinary people, most of them poor and unimportant (though they might not have agreed with that!). Nobody in the Middle Ages would have put them at the beginning of a book—more often than not, they were not included at all. All the same, everything depended on these folk and the work they did. Many of them were no doubt proud of their skills.

PEASANT

"Peasant" is an equal-opportunity job, open to men, women, and children. Do you like outdoors work and the challenge of changing weather and seasons? As a peasant farmer, you will work in the fields from dawn to dark in sun, rain, and snow. At different times of the year, you might pull a light plow, sow grain, scythe hay, trample grapes, shear sheep, herd pigs, gather firewood, or make and repair tools and huts.

You and your family may own your own small farm, but you worry about losing it. You always have to work on your lord's land before your own. In case of storm or flood, you must save your lord's crops first. You can hardly turn around without paying a fee to your lord—to grind grain in his mill or settle an argument in his court. You pay when his son is knighted or his daughter married or (worst of all) when he loses a fight and must be ransomed. The Church expects one-tenth of everything, your tax to God. Most peasants dig their land with a wooden hoe and spade. You try to grow two crops each year. Winters are bad. If you can't store enough grain or a thief steals your only pig, your family may starve.

In the fall, you might earn a few coppers (pennies) picking grapes and trampling them for wine. Men are paid twice as much as women for the same work. Not fair, huh? Your home may be a two-room hut with a hole in the roof to let out smoke, and straw-filled mattresses for beds. In winter, your pig, your sheep, and the hens move in with you. Often, you're too tired to think. You dream of living in a house with a thatched roof, windows, and a chimney, of owning a pot and a skillet, of eating at a table and sleeping on a feather bed.

If you own a plow and a horse or an ox, you are rich. If you are very rich, you may own land, plowhorses, sheep, pigs, cattle, perhaps a boat and net for fishing, a vineyard, a woodlot. Your son may marry the daughter of a poor squire. Then your grandchildren will be born as nobles, and you will have to curtsy or bow to them!

SERF

The serf's job is like the peasant's, only worse. You live and work on your lord's land; you can't move away. If the land is sold, you work for the new owner. Your lord has a duty to protect you from outlaws and feed you if the crops fail, but old people and babies often die. You are not a slave. Your lord cannot sell you, or hang you for no reason. If money grew on trees and you could pick some, you could buy a tiny piece of land.

You could buy your freedom, but then your lord wouldn't have to feed you in bad times. If you are brave and lucky, you can run away to town. You won't dare beg for food; that's a sure way to get caught, and then you may be dragged home and whipped. Your lord might mark you – maybe burn his brand on your face or cut off an ear. But if he doesn't catch you for a year and a day, you and your children and their children forever afterwards will be free.

A Medieval Breakthrough: The Heavy Plow

Does your family have a garden? Have you ever used a spade? If so, you'll know that not all soil is easy to dig. Today, a rototiller can turn over hard clay soil or cut through a tangle of roots. A big, modern, tractor-driven plow will go through almost anything.

Farmers in the Middle Ages didn't have power machinery. To get fields ready for planting, they used a light plow pulled by an ox or a horse or a person.

But much of the soil in northern Europe was too heavy and wet to be turned this way. So farmers welcomed two inventions: a heavy plow on wheels, and a new way of harnessing animals so that a team of six or eight oxen or horses could share the work of pulling it. After the heavy plow came into general use, peasant farmers could turn furrows in heavy soil; they could clear forests and drain swamps to produce bountiful harvests. Peasants had to work together, though. Even the richest peasant did not own more than one or two oxen.

BREWER; BREWSTER

This job was a money-maker for many women. In the early Middle Ages, you could brew ale at home, without any special equipment, and sell whatever your family did not need. You might develop your own one-woman business, the way a good cook today might begin by selling pies and cakes to the neighbors.

Later in the Middle Ages, brewsters of ale (women) were mostly replaced by brewers of beer (men), who learned the trade from Dutchmen who had moved to England. Unlike the woman who brewed ale part-time at home, a brewer of beer usually hired other workers and went into business full-time. When the business moved outside the home, often a man ran the show, although his wife and other women might brew the beer.

Scholars have naturally wondered why men took over the brewing trade. Part of the reason seems to have been the way records were kept. In the Middle Ages, a husband was head of the household, so he would automatically be recorded as the owner of a family business. If a single woman owned a brewing business, her name would be listed as the owner.

There were fines for giving a short measure of ale or beer and for using bad ingredients. A woman repeat offender might be put in the ducking stool and ducked in a river or lake; a man might be put in the stocks.

The suffix "ster" often means a woman's career:

brewster (female)
brewer (male)

webster (female)
weaver (male)

spinster (female)
spinner (male)

The old names of many of these occupations survive today as family names. If your name is Webster, some women in your family long ago were weavers; if it's Cutler, your ancestors sold or sharpened knives. Look in the index to this book to see if the last names of your family or friends are listed.

Phew! I am so parched.

MILLER

Everybody brings their grain for you to grind: rye or wheat for bread, malt barley for beer. You may build your mill beside a flowing stream, using a waterwheel to turn the huge round millstones. If there is no stream, oxen, horses, or humans tread around and around to turn the wheel.

Grain for peasants is coarse-ground, with some grit from the stones mixed in. Nobles insist on fine-ground wheat flour. Millers have a bad reputation for cheating; many of them charge for grinding and also keep some flour for themselves.

In the Middle Ages, there was no electric power or gasoline. Water and wind (along with gears) were sometimes used to provide power for grinding grain, tanning leather, laundering clothes, sawing wood, pressing olive oil, casting iron, mashing malt for beer and pulp for paper, and operating fullers' vats for finishing woollen cloth, bellows for blast furnaces, and hydraulic hammers for foundries.

BAKER; BAXTER

You start work before daylight, kneading the dough and setting it to rise; adding charcoal or wood to the firebox and raking the coals to adjust the heat; sliding your loaves into the giant oven and pulling your long wooden paddle out from under them with a quick jerk. Ordinary houses don't have ovens, so peasants and townsfolk bring bread and meat for special occasions to you for baking. (At home, bread or biscuits are usually baked in the ashes of the hearth fire.)

You and your apprentices and journeymen develop powerful arms from kneading dough: huge "knight's loaves," smaller "squire's loaves" and little "page's loaves," or rolls. You have your own specialties: two-color bread (with layers of wheat and rye), bread for trenchers (thick slices that are used instead of plates) or twice-baked bread (crackers). You sweat in summertime, but your bakery is warm when cold winds blow, and there's no finer smell than hot, fresh bread.

Your bakery is near a stream, and the boys fill your buckets every morning, but you always worry about fire. No sensible lord allows a bakery inside his castle walls. When there's a feast, servants have to run to the great hall with huge platters of baked food.

I sure am thirsty.

Guilds

When towns began to get rich, powerful nobles and churchmen wanted to control them. The nobles had big armies; the churchmen could refuse to marry, christen, or bury anybody in the towns that resisted them.

The townsfolk needed to work together. Then they could bargain with their powerful neighbors and buy freedom and protection. Over time, the towns developed their own spheres of influence; in limited ways, they functioned independently. So long as they did not get into a power struggle with nobles or church, they pretty much ruled themselves.

People in different occupations formed associations called "guilds." Guilds regulated the prices of goods, people's wages, the quality of products, the conditions under which people worked, and anything else to do with their own craft or trade. Guilds often ran the new city and town governments. Rich guilds took care of widows and orphans.

Craft guilds were ruled by "master craftsmen" who owned their own shops. Journeymen worked in their masters' shops and were paid by the day. To learn a craft, children—occasionally girls, but usually boys—were sent to work for masters. As apprentices, they received valuable training, along with food and a place to sleep. They worked hard but were not paid. Instead, their fathers or somebody else paid the master a fee.

How did you get to be master of a trade or craft? There were three steps: apprentice—journeyman—master (just as there were three steps to knighthood: page—squire—knight). An apprentice learned a trade and became a journeyman eventually but might never become a master, just as a squire might never become a knight.

Suppose you were a journeyman goldsmith who had served your apprenticeship (probably seven years) and learned your craft. When towns were just beginning, you could become a master by creating a "masterwork," a glorious two-handled chalice, perhaps, or a woman's golden belt. Of course, you had to provide the gold, unless you found a client who trusted you or your master agreed to help. As time went on, however, masters didn't want too many other masters in their guild. They didn't want to share their power, so they made more and more rules. Sometimes the only way for a capable journeyman to become a master was to marry his master's daughter.

City of London Guilds were called Livery Companies, because each one had its own livery, or uniform, which is still worn today on special occasions by members of the 75 surviving companies, including mercers (fabric dealers), drapers, merchant taylors (tailors), and other workers in the cloth trades; haberdashers (sellers of household supplies such as thread and tape, as well as caps and hats); grocers, fishmongers, and vintners (makers and sellers of wine); goldsmiths and ironmongers; salters and chandlers (makers of candles and soap).

Florence, in Italy, had 73 craft guilds in 1316. Cloth manufacturers, furriers, butchers, money changers, proprietors of public baths, sewer cleaners, garbage removers, and teachers of grammar, arithmetic, reading, and writing were a few of them. If I were going to be a sewer cleaner, I'd rather be a master than an apprentice. How about you?

SPINSTER; SPINNER

Medieval peasants wore simple clothes made of scratchy wool. Making clothes for the family is usually a do-it-yourself job, starting with shearing your own sheep, washing the fleece, and combing out all the tangles. Taking the clean wool and turning it into yarn is the spinster or spinner's part of the garment-making job. Women who spin yarn are spinsters; men are called spinners, but there aren't many of those. In a family business, a wife often spins yarn for her husband to weave into cloth. (Later, "spinster" came to mean an unmarried woman.)

To spin woollen fleece into yarn, first you wind a mass of fluffy wool around your distaff (a wooden rod with a forked end). Holding the distaff in one hand or under your arm, you pull some fiber out into a thread, twisting it as you pull. When your thread is long enough, you tie it to your spindle (shaped like a top, with a weight at the bottom), and give it a spin. The weight keeps the fibers pulling slowly through your fingers, and the turning action twists them into yarn. Late in the Middle Ages, spinning wheels began to replace distaffs and spindles, making spinning faster and easier.

WEAVER; WEBSTER

"Weaver" was one of the most important cloth-making jobs. In many cities, the Weavers' Guild was big and powerful. After 1000 CE, professional weavers would use horizontal looms, where you sit down and work a treadle with your feet to raise and lower lengthwise (warp) threads; then you slide the shuttle with the crosswise (weft) yarn back and forth. Many peasants still used the old vertical looms, where you stand up and weave your yarn in and out. Wool and linen were the common fabrics.

Noblewomen were often good weavers, supervising cloth-making in the castle. A woman who weaves is a webster; however, most weavers were men.

WALKER OR FULLER

By either name, your job is to finish the cloth after it comes off the loom. You use fuller's earth (a kind of clay) and urine to wet the warm woollen cloth, then you walk on it—on the wrong side. When you tramp on the fabric, the fibers rub against each other and twist into each other, so that the loosely woven cloth will firm up and keep its shape. The wet smelly cloth is stretched on a tenter to dry.

Tenters are huge wooden frames with a row of hooks at both ends to hold the fulled cloth. As it dries, the fabric tries to shrink; it pulls and strains against the hooks. Today, when you are waiting for important news (like getting your report card), you might say you're "on tenter-hooks." That means you are feeling like the woollen cloth.

A professional fuller needed a lot of urine. It came from both humans and animals. Women sometimes collected the family's urine to make extra money; schoolboys at one school urinated into a large bucket so that this urine could be sold. Did fullers have stinky feet? Probably, but one modern person who fulled cloth for a cloak using the medieval process reported his woollen cloth was wonderfully soft and not smelly at all.

CORDWAINER (SHOEMAKER)

As a cordwainer, you are an artist of the shoemaking world, creating fashionable, elegant footwear for royals and nobles or rich merchants from high-quality leather. The word "cordwainer" comes from Cordoba in Spain, where fine cordovan leather is made from the hide of moufflon goats. This luxurious leather was first brought back to England at the time of the Crusades.

The London Cordwainers' Guild was established before 1160; it still survives today. The coat of arms features the heads of four goats.

COBBLER

You make and repair shoes and other leather goods for ordinary people, often reusing bits and pieces. You make holes in your leather with a sharp awl, then hand-stitch it, often not very well. We still speak of a patchy job as something that's been "cobbled together."

BLACKSMITH

Your job is to make or repair iron objects, first by heating, then by hammering. You heat the metal in your forge, using charcoal or coke (coal residue) as fuel. When the iron is white-hot, you move it very carefully to an anvil and hammer it into shape: a hinge or horseshoe, perhaps a sword. Then you plunge the finished item into water to temper, or harden, it.

There is a kind of magic in the smith's work. Weyland the Smith, a strong man in Germanic legend, was a mythic character, said to have kept his smithy–his workshop—at various places in Germany and England. The swords he made never broke in battle. If you want muscles that all your friends will envy, be a smith!

CHANDLER

As the towns grew, merchants set up small shops. If you had a shop, you sold only one kind of product. Often, you made or grew your product as well as selling it. If you are a chandler, you make and sell two kinds of candles, as well as soap. Tallow candles are made from beef and sheep fat, rendered and poured into a mold. These candles are smelly, smoky, and quick-burning, but cheap. Beeswax candles burn well, but ordinary people can't afford them, even when the beekeeper doesn't drive a hard bargain for his empty honeycombs.

You make soap from the same fat as the tallow candles, boiling it and adding ashes. Your hands are red and raw from making soap, but your customers buy it all.

SALTER OR DRYSALTER

You produce and/or sell salt. It's a good business; everybody needs salt to keep meat and fish from spoiling during the winter or to make cabbages into sauerkraut, as well as enjoying it on their food.

Salt boilers make salt by boiling brine from natural springs (the brine may be eight times as salty as sea water). It takes two weeks to dry the lumps of salt; then they can be ground in a mill or cut into small blocks for sale. Salt mines are the other source of salt. Because everybody needs salt, kings often charge a sales tax on it when they want money for going to war.

FISHMONGER

To do this job, you must live close to a big river or the ocean. You sell fresh fish, which you buy every day at the docks. In London, Billingsgate is the biggest fish market. It's noisy, too, with vendors crying their wares—"Cockles and mussels, alive, alive-oh," "Live eels for sale" and all the rest. It's enough to make your head ache. But fish are cheap, and your shop is not far away.

You also prepare and sell salt fish, though the careful housewife saves her money and salts her own winter supply.

CHAPTER TWO
Religious Jobs

The religious jobs of the Middle Ages were concerned in one way or another with people's souls: saving or damning them in the hereafter. If you believed that your short life on earth was mainly preparation for your eternal life after death, as medieval Christianity preached, then those who had the jobs of helping you to get there—or hindering you—were very important.

The Jewish faith existed in medieval Europe. Small numbers of Jews quietly practiced their religion in many European cities, but they were never really safe. Spain, an Islamic country for 700 years, was wonderfully tolerant of different religious views, though Christianity eventually put an end to that. Far and away the biggest and most important religion was Christianity. The Christian church in Europe was the Catholic Church, and that was that!

However, not all Christians in the Middle Ages believed everything the Church wanted them to believe, even if they had to act that way. Kings sometimes had to obey the orders of the pope, though not always happily. But sometimes the pope did what a king wanted, even though he didn't exactly say so.

There were many ranks and varieties of careers for clergy in the Church. The top power jobs were pope, cardinal, and bishop. There were two popes for part of the 14th and 15th centuries, one in Rome and one in Avignon, which was controlled by France. The pope in Avignon excommunicated the pope in Rome and all his followers. The pope in Rome excommunicated the pope in Avignon and all his followers. Each pope claimed to be supreme head of the Catholic Church. Each pope had cardinals, bishops, and priests, as well as a huge office staff. Each pope lived in luxury in a great palace. Each pope collected money. This was very confusing. How could anybody know for sure who was the true pope? If you chose the wrong one, causing the right one to excommunicate you, then you would surely fall into the Devil's power when you died. But while this situation lasted, there were twice as many top jobs in the Church!

Some monks and nuns had special jobs in their abbeys, often similar to jobs in the outside world, such as:

- Almoner: distributed food or other help to the sick and poor

- Cellarer: had charge of all the property, rents, and revenues of the abbey, supervised the servants and lay brethren, and bought supplies

- Chamberlain: provided clothes, shoes, and bedding for the monks and other workers

- Infirmarian: cared for the sick and elderly in the infirmary

- Kitchener: oversaw preparation of meals

- Novice-Master: prepared people who wanted to become monks or nuns

- Precentor: had books ready for the many different services and prayers throughout each day

- Prior/Prioress or Sub-Prior: second-in-command to the abbot or abbess, having general oversight of the abbey and everybody in it

- Sacrist: in charge of security and cleaning in the abbey church, including vessels for the altar

- Succentor: in charge of the library, and also of music and chanting in the abbey church

POPE

As head of the Church, the pope has more power than any king; he is second only to God. He is a leader in matters of faith, such as determining proper beliefs, and also in practical matters, such as administering a huge organization and working to bring about "right order" in the world.

Pope St. Gregory VII (b. between 1020 and 1025, d. 1085) was probably the most influential medieval leader of the Church. He believed the church had to take action to bring about right order, thus paving the way for Pope Urban II to call for a crusade to capture Jerusalem, and laying the groundwork for centuries of warfare in the name of religion.

How can you become pope? You must be an able and dedicated priest and astute politician, from a good family, most often Italian. But you'll still need luck to be ready at the right time. This is a lifetime job, so a new pope can only be chosen when the old pope dies. Even with luck, you might spend most of your life preparing for this position, and only a few years as pope.

CARDINAL

In the early Middle Ages, the most important priest in any big, important church might be called a cardinal; as time passed, the title was reserved for cardinals in and near Rome. It is a big job, second only to that of pope. Cardinals are the equals of kings, outranking bishops and archbishops.

As a cardinal, you may dine with royalty, exchange gifts with them and attend royal events. More important, though, is your place as "the power behind the throne." Frequently, you can arrange matters so that the king's council acts as you think best. You manage church affairs and discipline and the church courts in your area. You also assist the pope, sometimes in matters of faith and discipline, sometimes in practical matters, such as organizing a crusade or raising money. Over time, you and your fellow cardinals will acquire the responsibility of choosing the next pope.

BISHOP

Do you ever have problems because your mom wants you to behave one way, and your dad another? Do you ever get caught between what your teacher expects and your parents demand? If so, you know that having two bosses can be difficult. Bishops in the Middle Ages had two powerful bosses: the king and the pope.

If you are a bishop, you usually hold lands and property from the king and swear homage and fealty to him as your liege lord. You may follow him into battle and fight at his side. However, your official job is to be a leader in the Church, responsible for the spiritual well-being of priests and people in your diocese (church area) and administering church property. In this important job, your boss is the pope. Often, pope and king make very different demands. The king and the pope have to agree about appointing you, but in a rich diocese, you are probably more loyal to the king.

ABBOT; ABBESS

As abbot or abbess, you are the head of your religious community. (The prior or prioress is second in command.) If you are an able leader, you can achieve great power, including membership on the king's council.

Other power roles exist for men, but abbess is the most powerful job a noblewoman can hold in religious life. If you undertake this career, you may rule a convent as big as a city, with 5,000 or 6,000 people, though 100 to 500 was more usual. Nuns, novices (women hoping to become nuns), and lay sisters (other women who serve the community) live inside the convent walls; men at arms may be housed just outside. The convent usually has quarters for visitors and for male clerics. It has an infirmary or hospital for sick people, herb and vegetable gardens, and often fish ponds (you eat more fish than meat). Outside the walls are fields where peasants grow other food for the community. Even though you delegate supervision to others as much as possible, you are in charge of everything.

FRIAR

You are a wandering religious man, belonging to a holy order. Francis of Assisi started the Franciscan order of monks. He preached to the birds, who seemed to listen to his sermons.

Francis believed that monks should go into the world and care for lepers and beggars, but friars did not always live up to the high ideals of their orders. Friar Tuck was one of Robin Hood's band of outlaws. Medieval stories depict him in much the same way modern films do: a jolly fellow, fighting with others more often than rescuing them.

PARSON

You are a poor country priest. Your job includes celebration of mass, baptism for new-borns, and last rites for the dying; giving advice and comfort—or a warning to mend wicked ways; visiting people in their homes; and teaching the village children. Nobody else in the village can read and write.

The poet Chaucer described the perfect parson, someone who would rather give away his own property than squeeze donations from the poor. In sickness or grief, families called on this parson and he came, through rain and thunder, however far away they lived. This good man was not proud of his goodness, and he did not despise sinners.

MONK, NUN

You live a strict life with others of your order, withdrawn from the outside world. Your days include long periods of prayer and silence. You

fast often; you wear simple clothes. Usually, you try this life as a novice for several years before taking your vows.

Sometimes even the most religious woman cannot take full vows unless she donates money or property. However, she can still live and work in the abbey. A monk who donates property can expect a better position than a poor man. Ability does count in these jobs, though. A big abbey, monastery, or convent is like a town; it needs cooks and gardeners, almoners and medics, masons and carpenters, and peasants to work the fields. Some abbeys specialize in making books, others in healing the sick or making a special liqueur or cordial.

The monks of Meteora, in Greece, lived in monasteries on top of huge, jagged spikes of stone, so steep that people and supplies had to be drawn up by rope ladders. They certainly lived apart from the world! Today, you can visit their ancient monasteries. Some monks still live there, though they don't talk to tourists.

CHAPLAIN

You may be the resident priest of a castle or manor house or of a chapel, or you may do your duty in a monastery. Whatever the case, you are in charge of the religious observances of the household. Sometimes your job also includes teaching some of the children. If you see bad behavior, even in your lord and lady, it is your duty to take them to task, perhaps even to assign a penance (an act to show regret). But beware: although your sacred position should protect you from their anger, it doesn't always.

The Franciscans (monks) made vows of poverty and went into the world, preaching and caring for outcasts and sick people. The Poor Clares (nuns) wanted to do the same, but they could not get permission from the pope to live and work outside their abbey walls because they were women. However, outcasts and sick people came to them.

FIGHTING CLERICS

The Templars and the Hospitallers

The two great passions of the Middle Ages were religion and war. In the Knights Templar and the Hospitallers—fighting monks—these passions were combined. Both orders were under the direct authority of the pope, and they could not be taxed or controlled by any king. The Templars especially became rich and proud. Having dedicated their lives, they accepted every risk in battle. They were usually the first to advance and the last to retreat. When captured, they refused to be ransomed, choosing rather to be executed by their enemies.

If you join one of these orders, your job will be to live in the Holy Lands and defend them after the crusaders go home. Your job is a mixture of monk and warrior. Your home is a fortified monastery. You wear a monastic habit marked with a cross and participate in all religious duties; in battle, you wear a red surcoat with a white cross over your armor.

CHAPTER THREE
Castle Jobs

The lord of the castle was the boss, but everybody shared in his importance and high standing, from his lady wife and their children down to the turnspit in the kitchen, who lorded it over his peasant family. The lord of a castle might be a king, baron, duke, count, or other nobleman, or a knight with no other title. As we've seen, society was organized like a pyramid, with the king at the top and the peasants at the bottom. Individual castles and manors were pyramids too, only smaller, with the lord at the top, and the peasants on his estate at the bottom. Many other people came in between.

On a big estate, jobs were specialized. A master ewerer (in charge of the hand-washing arrangements at dinner, and of the table linens) might have half a dozen workers whose only job was to help with the tablecloths. (Imagine that!) On a small estate, one person might do several jobs. Always, your duty was to serve your lord. If you were part of his household, your lord's duty to you was to provide protection, work, shelter, and food, clothing, and sometimes pay.

No service to your lord was beneath your dignity, because it did not change your place in the social structure. A great baron might wait at table, serving his king. A titled lady-in-waiting might help dress the baron's wife or daughter, or empty their chamber pots. This chapter lists some jobs under a general heading of "domestic servants." Many of these people (or their parents or grandparents) came from peasant families.

The feudal system depended on knightly honor. A true knight valued his honor more than his life. However, some rules of knightly honor are hard to understand. A knight might promise safety to hostages if their city surrendered, then hang the hostages anyway on some flimsy excuse. Perhaps he had not sworn "on my honor as a knight," or perhaps he claimed treachery by someone else in the town. Knights were supposed to defend maidens and protect the powerless. Sometimes they did, especially if the maidens were beautiful and the powerless people were rich. In England, *Magna Carta*, a political charter, protected ordinary people better than knights did. On the continent of Europe, peasants were almost slaves; far from protecting them, nobles did not even see peasants as people like themselves.

Nobles married to extend their families' property and power (like mergers of big companies today). A couple might be engaged before they were 10 years old and married by age 15! Sometimes they met for the first time on their wedding day. Many couples loved each other, but love came after marriage, not before.

Nobles had big families. More noble babies than peasant babies lived to grow up, maybe because they enjoyed better food and care. Noble dads didn't change diapers or help with feeding. Disposable diapers and formula would not be invented for hundreds of years. Babies were breast-fed, but not always by their mothers. Many noble babies were sent out to be cared for by peasant women with babies of their own.

PAGE

As a child of about seven or eight years old, your parents send you to live with another noble family, to serve as a page and learn to become a knight.

For the next six years, you help your lord to bathe and dress, take care of his clothes, and wait on him at table. You learn to ride, fight, and hunt with hawks; to play chess and backgammon; to sing and dance, play an instrument and compose music. The lord's chaplain teaches religious education, along with a little reading and writing, most of which you quickly forget. Who cares if a knight can read?

SQUIRE

At 14 or 15, you become a squire and begin serious training for combat. You joust at the quintain (piercing a swinging dummy with your lance); fight with sword, battle-ax, and mace; and study the rules of jousting and heraldry. You lead your lord's warhorse into combat and hold it when he fights on foot. At home, you still dress your lord and wait on him, but you also do many other useful tasks. Your lord trusts you to keep his keys, carry his purse, or deliver confidential messages. You can't read much, but your memory never lets you down, even if a message is long and complicated.

In earlier days, you might have been knighted because of brave deeds. You didn't need a lot of money. Now, if you are poor, you may be a squire all your life, unless perhaps you save your lord's life or unhorse a knight in combat, winning equipment and a ransom.

Grrr!

KNIGHT

You rule your lands and administer justice. However, fighting in battles or tournaments is your main work.

You are proud of your strength and endurance, which allow you to ride all day, sleep on the ground, then fight in blazing sun or snowstorms without much food or water. At a gallop, fully armed, you can hit a small moving target with a lance as long as a full-size car. You can ride and fight wearing 25 kilograms (55 pounds) of armor, a two-handed sword hanging from your belt on one side and a long dagger on the other, and a battle-ax, longer sword, or club-headed mace attached to your saddle. You and your warhorse are a medieval one-horsepower tank.

At home, you and your lady wife go hunting and hawking, and entertain your neighbors with feasts. You hold court, mete out justice, buy a second warhorse, admire the new baby (a son), and order armor, the new style with plate instead of a chain-mail shirt. Maybe you fight in a tournament or two, or plan a daughter's marriage to enlarge your estates. Soon, however, you fret for war. Perhaps you will join a crusade to the Holy Land.

From the highest nobility to the lowest, knights loved fighting; they spent their lives training to fight, then fighting in tournaments or war. They must have been very strong to ride and fight in their armor of chain-mail or plate, covering chest, arms, and legs: a chain-mail skirt over a chain-mail shirt and padded tunic, chain-mail or heavy leather gauntlets on their hands, and a dark, stuffy helmet weighing three to five kilograms (six to eleven pounds), on their heads. Over everything, they wore a tunic embroidered with their coat of arms.

Knights rode with very long stirrups, almost standing up. They had amazing control of their horses and weapons. Three great lords served the royal dinner at the coronation of King Charles VI of France while riding prancing horses and balancing the plates of food on the end of their lances!

From watching television, you might think a knight spent his working days knocking down other knights in tournaments, fighting battles, or rescuing lovely ladies. Those were the ideals of chivalry: honor, protecting the weak, keeping your word, battling to the death in a good cause. In real life, battle armor rusted in the rain, tournament helmets cut off vision, and a knight did not hesitate to besiege an enemy castle because ladies lived in it, or to take them prisoner if the castle fell.

Tournaments

Tournaments lasting a week or more were the great sporting events of the Middle Ages. Everybody came. Glittering ladies and lords filled the central stands, showing off their jewelled clothes of crimson and green and cloth of gold. Merchants and tradespeople, artisans, entertainers, food vendors, and pickpockets ("cutpurses") crowded in. Trumpets sounded, and the parade began. The knights wore special armor, sparkling with gold, brightly painted with their colors and emblems. Plumes swayed on their helmets. Their warhorses champed on golden bridles. Two squires on horseback, an armorer, and several men on foot followed each knight. Two kinds of events took place: jousts, where one knight fought another, and group fights or melées. In addition to their entertainment value, tournament fights were an imitation of battle: they offered experience to young knights and kept older knights in practice. Organizers set up the matches very carefully so that the younger knights would mostly fight each other and champions would not eliminate each other early in the contest.

Tournaments were horrendously expensive. As well as fancy armor and outfits for the parade, a knight had to provide fine clothes for himself and his family to wear at banquets and other special events. If he lost, he had to pay a ransom, and he also lost his horse and armor, though he could sometimes buy them back. In a single tournament, a knight could ruin himself and his family.

HERALD

At tournaments, you are master of ceremonies, judge, and referee. You pair knights to make sure they are evenly matched. You announce combats, start and (sometimes) stop them. You make rulings; for example, if someone is eligible to fight. You know the names, badges, emblems, colors, and devices of a huge number of noble families (including yours), as well as the most obscure rules for different kinds of fights.

In war, you may carry formal messages and sometimes even negotiate on behalf of your lord. This is supposed to be a safe job; however, some short-tempered nobles haven't heard the medieval version of "Don't kill the messenger."

ARMORER

It's your job to make and repair arms and armor. In peacetime, you prepare your lord's armor for tournaments. In time of war, you go with him. You carry your tools and equipment, even your forge, so that you can repair a sword or a chain-mail shirt or make more spearheads as needed.

The woman warrior

Joan of Arc was not the only great fighting woman of the Middle Ages. In the 1100s, Queen Matilda led an invasion and defeated King Stephen of England. The French Countess of Montfort took command in 1341 when her husband was captured. Under siege, she led the defense in full armor astride a warhorse. She ordered the townswomen to cut their long skirts and carry stones and pots of boiling pitch to throw down on the enemy. After her husband died, she went on fighting, although the English finally captured and imprisoned her. Other women of the time also fought, defended castles, and negotiated peace.

NOBLEWOMAN

As wife and mother, you have charge of the household, sometimes several hundred people. When your husband is at war, you are his deputy. You control his men and property, negotiating marriages, punishing wrongdoers, and acting in every way on his behalf. The bailiff reports to you.

You read and write both Latin and French, and have studied astronomy, household management, and elements of medicine and first aid. You are proud of your embroidery and tapestries, and you teach these skills to your daughters and your ladies. Your arrow sometimes hits the mark, but you'd rather hawk than hunt. You can defend the castle in a siege or protect your family's interests under the law. You read every day from your Book of Hours, a special prayer book; and often from books of etiquette, home remedies, and law.

PRINCESS

Was "princess" a career? You be the judge!

You dream of being the wife and mother of kings, advising the ruler or even ruling the land yourself if your husband dies while your son is a child. You take for granted the luxuries of splendid food, rich clothes, and many servants. Your heavy jewelled dresses tire you out, and your slashed-velvet sleeves are too stiff for hunting or archery. You have companions, but no real friends. You have read about princesses who fought for their lands. You could do the same, but you usually get your way without a fight.

You will be engaged next month to a man you have never seen, and so far, you can't find out anything about him except his name. Your cousin Princess Elizabeth of Hungary (1207–30) was engaged at 4 and married at 14, and you will soon turn 13, so it's time. Some princesses are betrothed at birth. Will your husband be young and handsome, or old and ugly? Cruel or kind? It doesn't matter. Your father will make sure that your husband's lands are rich and his family is powerful, and you will be his loyal and obedient wife until death parts the two of you, because that's your job.

Books for women showed how to make ink, get rid of fleas, use chicken feathers to remove grease stains, care for pet birds, make spiced wine, or defend a castle. Books told how to train servants, give alms to the poor, or walk modestly in public, not "with roving eyes and neck stretched forth like a stag in flight." However, there were no books on baby and child care.

BAILIFF

(also called REEVE or STEWARD)

By any of these names, you are the foreman of the manor, the lord's representative. Whatever needs doing, it's your job to see that it gets done right, without waste, and on time: from spring plowing and seeding to fall harvest, from repairing buildings to collecting fees and rents, to having the peasants' sheep driven into your lord's sheep-fold at night, so that he gets the manure. Every peasant works without pay for the lord three or four days each week; you assign their jobs, see that everyone does a good day's work and make sure nothing is stolen or misused. You keep records of the money you collect and spend, and you may hold court and dispense justice.

This important job often attracts bullies and rogues. As a reeve or bailiff, you have power over many peasants, and if you are dishonest there are opportunities to cheat your noble employer as well as the poor folk. You might charge extra fees and keep the money, accuse an innocent person of theft and demand a bribe to let her go, or even protect local bandits in exchange for part of their loot. If you keep good order on the estate and turn over enough money, your lord might not care about your unscrupulous side deals. I hope you'll choose to be an honest bailiff, though!

CONSTABLE; MARSHAL

You are the chief officer of a noble household or royal court. You direct the whole operation, like the CEO (Chief Executive Officer) of a big business today. You are the

lord's deputy; you speak and act for him when he is away or in poor health. If you are English, you may hope to serve your king as Constable of England.

As marshal, your job is similar, but more limited: you direct the military forces, especially the cavalry. In a smaller household, you look after transport, including horses, carts, and wagons; you supervise grooms, blacksmiths, farriers (who put shoes on the horses) and record-keeping clerks.

FALCONER

FALCONER; MASTER OF FALCONRY

Hunting birds or small animals with trained falcons is the favorite sport of many noble lords and ladies. They value the falconer who captures, trains, and cares for their hawks. Sometimes you climb the cliffs to take young birds from their nests; sometimes you capture full-grown wild birds. These older birds are better hunters but can never be completely tamed. You know the five falcons most often used in the hunt, though the great gyrfalcon and the swift peregrine are your favorites; a peasant can be hanged for keeping one of these.

You know more about keeping your birds healthy than most doctors know about people. You make jesses (leg straps) and hoods for the falcons, and leather gloves worn by owners or handlers; you can repair any harness on the spot during a hunt. When your lord goes to war, you and your hawks may go with him to hunt for food.

ARCHER

You shoot with bow and arrows at a target, at animals in the hunt, or at enemies in battle. Duke William of Normandy conquered England in 1066 when he ordered his archers to aim high into the air. An arrow hit King Harold of England in the eye and killed him.

As an English archer, you use the longbow, made of yew, longer than a person is tall. You can shoot 10 or 12 80 cm-long (31.5-inch) arrows in a minute, compared to two from a crossbow, and hit a target 200 meters (650 feet) distant. In battle, you often aim high, and enjoy a grim chuckle when your arrows hit the horses' rumps and the beasts rear and snort. If your arrow downs a knight, you may get a share of his ransom.

Most English commanders aren't glory hogs. They place you where your deadly arrows can do the most damage and don't hesitate to praise you, though often enough they never get around to paying your wages. With a bit of luck, however, you may take home enough money to buy a farm. The French knights think it's disgraceful to owe victory to common men, so they hold their archers back. Often, their crossbow men don't let loose more than one or two bolts. So much the better for you!

JESTER OR FOOL

You are the stand-up comic of the Middle Ages, entertaining royalty or other nobles on demand. You can poke fun at anybody or anything, but only as long as your master laughs. You need quick wits and a wicked sense of humor, along with the good judgment to stop in time. You like to live on the edge. You make fun of others, but they also make fun of you. You're a storyteller, juggler, actor, and mimic, as well as a jokester, shifting gears in a flash.

Everybody recognizes you, in your motley costume, your tri-pointed hat with bells, and your shoes with long, turned-up toes. It's a good life while it lasts.

ALMONER

Your job is to give small gifts of food, money, or other freebies to poor people, beggars, or the sick. During a noble person's pilgrimage, you walk alongside, throwing coins to the cheering crowd. At feasts, a portion of food is saved for you to distribute to poor people. Sometimes you live in an abbey or a town, instead of a castle. Churches and abbeys usually have food if people come at the right time, a bit like a Food Bank today. In the towns, guilds also give alms.

CHAMBERLAIN

You are the principal gentleman of the lord's bedchamber. Even for a powerful noble like you, it is an honor to help your lord get up and dress. You are the first to greet him in the morning, and the last to bid him goodnight. Often, your lord meets with a few trusted advisers before he gets up; you are always part of these meetings. Because you are so close to your lord, all the people who want something from him come to you for help.

zzz

Uh ... my lord,

... it's half twelve, my lord.

BUTLER

You are in charge of the cellar with its butts, or casks, of wine (usually 573 liters or 126 imperial gallons, per cask) and only slightly smaller casks of ale. These casks are huge, but the tops cannot easily be removed. You've heard that the Duke of Clarence was drowned in a butt of malmsey (a sweet wine), when he was imprisoned in the Tower of London. Your staff includes brewers, tapsters (who tap into the casks and draw out the liquor), and cupbearers.

How goes the feast?

They are about to serve the Blackbird pie.

DOMESTIC SERVANTS

From royal castles to manor houses, a typical noble family fed and housed as many servants as possible. A big retinue showed how important a noble was. For a peasant, any castle job was better than the fields. The lowly turnspits were proud to work in the baron's kitchen, although they spent hot, monotonous hours turning the roast to cook evenly over the fire.

The lady of a fairly small castle might have 20 maids. One or two of these were daughters of petty nobles, the others carefully chosen from peasant families. To be a maid, you will be trained to clean the rooms, to wipe down the stools and benches, to feed the lady's dogs and caged birds, to weave and sew and do other tasks.

If there are 20 maids, there are at least as many gardeners, footmen, regular kitchen staff, carpenters, and grooms, as well as masters of falconry and the hunt, of forests and waters, of bakery, cellar, furnishings, and various other specialties. If relatives or other people of rank live in the castle, they have their servants as well.

Here is a medieval recipe for poached salmon. If you read it out loud, you'll understand more of it than if you try to read it silently. Read "u" and "v" the way they sounded in the Middle Ages (the reverse of today) to make sense: e.g., vppon=upon; serue=serve. Notice how Roman numerals are used for the numbers: ii=2; iii=3.

The medieval cook began with the whole fish. Today, if you wanted to make this dish, you could buy two or three salmon fillets and go on from there to grill or barbecue them (on your gridiron) while you boiled some water and seasoned it with parsley and salt. You'd put the salmon pieces in the boiling water and let them simmer, then lift them out and put them in a dish to cool, decorating them with parsley dipped in vinegar. The recipe does not say how long you'd grill the fillets or boil them. You would need to know that fish cooks quickly!

SALMON FRESSH BOYLED

Take a fresh Salmon, and drawe him in the bely; and chyne him as a swine, and leche him flatte with a knife; and kutte the chyne in ii or iii peces, and roste him on a faire gredryn; & make faire sauce of water, parcelly, and salt. And whan hit begynneth to boyle, skem it clene, and cast the peces of salmon there-to, and lete hem seethe; and then take hem vppe, and lete hem kele, and ley a pece or ii in a dish; and wete faire foiles of parcely in vinegre, and caste hem vppon the salmon in the dish; and then ye shall serue hit.

COOK; PASTRY CHEF

A feast demands master cooks with pizzazz: artists who can sculpt castles out of butter; or prepare roasted swans and peacocks with feathers reattached and gilded beaks and feet, in fields of spun sugar and painted pastry; or make huge pies with live birds inside (four-and-twenty blackbirds, just like the nursery rhyme). The cockatrice is another spectacular creation, half suckling pig, half fowl, sewn together. You can create golden food by painting meat and fish with a mixture of egg yolk, saffron, and flour mixed with gold leaf. Alas, your masterworks, worthy of a museum, are demolished in one meal.

Fifty people might help prepare a feast, from the master chef and the wine steward down to the scullions who scour the pots.

A Medieval Feast

Most medieval cooking, for rich and poor alike, was so bland that people today wouldn't enjoy eating it. (This is partly because so much of it was boiled.) For a feast, however, cooks and their many helpers prepared food that looked amazing, even if it did not taste interesting. Everybody worked to make the feast a great event. Your lord's reputation for hospitality depended on you!

On special occasions, peasants on the estate were invited to feast on meats, bread, and ale outdoors at trestle tables, while higher-class people ate fancier food in the great hall. Inside and out, people were seated according to their rank, with the lord and lady and the most important nobles at a long table on a platform, looking down at everybody else. The high nobles might eat from gold or silver plates, but most people used thick slices of bread, called trenchers. Forks didn't come into use until almost the end of the Middle Ages; you hacked off meat with your own sharp knife, or scooped food from a dish and ate it with your fingers.

CHAPTER FOUR

Wonder Workers' Jobs

You may think—many people do—that everything in the Middle Ages was rough and crude compared to today. After all, they didn't have electricity or gasoline engines; they didn't have television or computers; they didn't even have radios or typewriters or kerosene lamps. How could they observe their world without microscopes or telescopes, or build huge, solid structures without modern ways to measure or weigh their materials?

How could they build elaborate engines of war, such as the trebuchet? This giant catapult's effectiveness depended on the meshing of five factors, each one of which could be changed: the weight of the stone ball; the length of the throwing sling; the counterweight design; the distance from the castle walls; and whether or not the whole massive structure was built with wheels. Experts have tried to reconstruct a trebuchet, based on ancient descriptions and pictures, using tools from that time; the project has been a huge challenge. How could engineers of the Middle Ages possibly get it right?

But they did. Some people of that time worked as precisely and accurately as an astronomer or a research scientist today. Some of them worked at the jobs in this chapter. They brought imagination and skill, originality and vision, to their work. The creations they left to us are now, centuries later, among the great treasures of our world.

Masters were well paid by standards of the day. A master mason or master carpenter in London around 1400 received eight pence for a day's work, from sunup to sunset. With one day's wages, he could buy 36 liters (8 gallons) of milk, or 2 kilograms (4 pounds) of butter, or 8 kilograms (32 cups) of salt, but he'd have to work for a week to buy 1.5 kilograms (6 cups) of sugar or 4 meters (4 yards) of good linen cloth. He would work for a whole day to buy as much sugar as a mason or carpenter could buy today with one and a half minutes' work.

INVENTOR

Can you imagine new things and figure out ways of building them? Be an inventor! The compass, mechanical clock, spinning wheel, treadle loom, windmill, and watermill were some medieval inventions, along with the heavy plow and ways of harnessing animals so that they shared the load.

ARTIFICER

As a technician, you make things that work, such as stage machinery for plays: a hell mouth belching flames, for example, or a harness for an angel to descend from heaven. Your best customer, though, might be a rich lord who loves practical jokes. He'd keep you busy creating booby traps in his castle, maybe starting with a hidden trap door in his bedroom. You'd also enjoy making toys for his children, such as miniature windmills that turn in the wind, or doll carriages that are harnessed to mice.

ARCHITECT

The great, glorious buildings of the Middle Ages were the cathedrals, with their pointed arches, flying buttresses, and vaulted ceilings. This was a new style of building, made possible partly because of Arabic numerals and decimal mathematics from the Islamic world, used by Christian architects to the glory of their God.

After years of training, study, and experience, you may rise to be an architect's assistant, then a master; and you may at last have the honor of designing a cathedral and supervising the building of it. If the money holds out and there's no war to interrupt the project, this will be your work for the rest of your life, and your son's work after you.

CHARTRES CATHEDRAL

You've heard the old joke, "Can you see the butter fly?" So, how about the buttress? To see flying buttresses, search the Internet for Chartres Cathedral, or go directly to **http://www.bc.edu/bc_org/ avp/cas/fnart/arch/chartres.html** for views and plans of Chartres Cathedral in France, built from 1194 to 1260, as well as glorious photos of the stained-glass windows. Another good site is Great Buildings Online, which shows the cathedral's floor plan and scale: **www.greatbuildings.com/gbc/ buildings/Chartres_Cathedral.html**

STONEMASON

Your grandfather built dry-stone walls to mark farm boundaries. His stones are fitted so carefully that they'll never shift, although he used no mortar. He was your first teacher. Even as a boy, however, you longed to cut and fit the stones of great buildings. You were apprenticed to a master who taught you to cut and fit, and also to measure and calculate. You traveled to Paris, and then to Moorish Spain, to study buildings and learn from masters there.

At last, you became a master yourself; now you are in charge of many workers building a cathedral, including carters and carpenters, painters and plumbers, as well as other masons. You can do fine work, carving a delicate lattice or a hideous gargoyle, but the great blocks of stone are your true passion.

ENGINEER

You design and build "engines" of war. In earlier times, the only way to capture a well-built castle was to starve out the defenders, but your work has changed all that. You build a tower higher than the castle walls, shielding it with wet animal skins so that flaming arrows can't set it on fire when you move in close. From it, your archers shoot down on the defenders, or you throw a bridge across the parapet. With the mighty trebuchet, you catapult huge stones to breach the castle walls, or send enormous boulders crashing into the midst of troops, animals, and peasant families inside. You direct miners who tunnel under the castle walls. As an engineer, you don't have noble rank or status, but it's your expertise and your siege engines that compel the garrison to surrender.

Of course, the defenders may shoot flaming arrows to fire your tower or trebuchet, though you shield the tower and mount the trebuchet on wheels, only moving it into range when ready to attack. Enemy engineers may discover your tunnel and build one to meet it; then there's a deadly struggle underground.

GOLDSMITH

In some towns all the metalworkers (goldsmiths, silversmiths, blacksmiths, and others) belong to the same guild: the Hammermen. However, the goldsmiths in your town have their own guild. Some goldsmiths buy all their gold, but you'd rather buy ore from miners; you make more money by extracting the gold yourself, and you don't have to test it for purity.

You beat the precious metal into sheets and create golden plates and goblets for Milord, or a necklace for Milady, or a golden screen for the cathedral. Count Robert has ordered a new drinking cup, but he hasn't paid for the last one, and he's had it for three years. If you could collect all the money your noble customers owe you, you would be rich. Merchants don't order such expensive items, but they pay on time.

COPYIST (SCRIBE)

You copy books letter by letter on vellum or parchment pages made from animal skins. Sometimes you illustrate every page with a border and decorated letters; more often, you copy the letters and an artist called an illuminator does the rest.

You work beside other monks or nuns in the abbey's scriborium, or in a workroom in a town. You (or your assistant) make and sharpen your own goose-quill pens and mix your oak-gall ink. The scriborium is cold and damp; your bones ache all winter. However, you do work indoors. You may not understand the language or care about the subject of the books you copy, but somebody else may work wonders with them.

BOOKBINDER

The first part of your job is to put the vellum pages for a new book in order. Then you stitch the sheets together, reinforce the spine with vellum, and glue the book to its cover. You make the covers from oak boards covered with tooled leather, with leather hinges and gold clasps to keep the book closed. Your finest covers glitter with jewelled panels of gold, silver, or ivory, as rich as your client will pay for. Sometimes a book is so big and heavy you have to make a special stand for it, with wheels so that it can be moved.

Some books are still bound by monks, but you have your own shop in Paris.

PARCHMENT AND INK SELLER

Your shop is the office supply center of the Middle Ages. You make and sell vellum and parchment, using animal skins; it's a smelly process. Near the end of the period, you may even stock a newfangled product: paper. You may hire a crier to advertise your wares in the street, calling, "Goose-quill pens, knife and whetstone, best prices in London! Real oak-gall ink, highest quality; never fades. Good white vellum. Buy it here!"

Some ink recipes have survived. This one is messy and sticky, but it doesn't take weeks of boiling, pounding, and drying, and the ingredients aren't hard to find. You mix egg white with soot, and add honey to make a smooth paste. If you print something with this ink, let the page dry, then put it in a clear vinyl case or cover it with plastic wrap so that it won't smudge.

Euclid lived in Greece and Egypt long ago, almost 2,000 years before the end of the Middle Ages. The great mathematician wrote in Greek. However, the first European translations of his books were not from old Greek into Latin. They were translations from Arabic! Maybe a copyist who did not understand Arabic copied a text that a scholar translated into Medieval Latin, and an architect who could read Latin used Euclid's geometry to build a cathedral.

Abbeys and noble families lent and borrowed books for copying—luckily for us, since fire, war, accident, and censorship have destroyed so many volumes, and those that survived were often damaged. Pages missing from one copy of a book might be complete in another.

There were no automatic spell checkers, although copyists often checked each other's work. If you made a mistake, others usually copied your mistake, even if it made nonsense of that part of the book. If several copies of the book exist today, scholars can often figure out who made the mistake!

Students could not usually buy their college textbooks. You would have to rent a section, copy it, then return it and rent the next part until you'd copied everything.

CHAPTER FIVE

Life and Death Jobs

Most medieval jobs varied with class and status. What you could or could not do, how you lived, what you might earn, had more to do with your place in society than with how good you were at your work. Health care was no different.

If you were a peasant or poor person, you knew better than to send for a doctor. No doctor would enter your hut. There were no drug companies and no insurance plans, no anesthetics, no sterile operating rooms or instruments, no X-rays, no lasers. Nobody knew about germs, about bacteria or microbes or bacilli, or even about how blood circulated in the human body. Because they didn't know, people tended to be superstitious, and they were suspicious about new treatments.

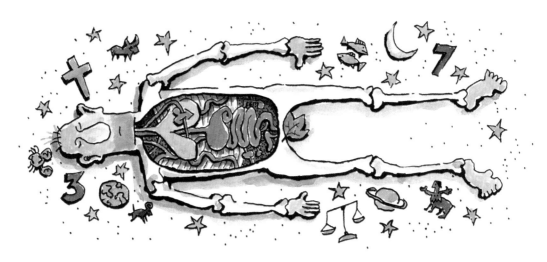

Abbeys and other church institutions built hospitals and cared for some people who otherwise would have died, but you had no right to be taken in anywhere; it was more a matter of luck.

People with disabilities were generally accepted in the Middle Ages, perhaps because so many conditions that would be corrected today were not then: for example, harelips, clubfeet, poor vision or hearing. Most people were not physically perfect. Crooked teeth were normal. When your toothache wouldn't stop, the barber-surgeon pulled a tooth or two. Wounds left ugly scars. Broken bones often healed crooked. Mentally disabled people could sometimes work well in fields or shops. "Simple" folk were accepted too. People believed God made everybody, after all.

BARBER; BARBER-SURGEON

Your job is to cut hair or bodies; that is, shave beards, pull teeth, set broken bones, or bleed your patients. (People believed that having too much blood caused many illnesses, so bloodletting was a common practice.) Yours is a craft, not a profession; you began as an apprentice and learned on the job.

Your shop is often dirty, and you don't always wash your hands or your tools between pulling Sam's tooth and his daughter Jenny's. You have no anesthetics, no bright lights or lasers, no electricity for drills or saws. Your apprentices hold down your patients when you set broken bones or amputate limbs; your work is easier when they faint from pain.

BLOODLETTING

If you were sick enough to send for a leech in the Middle Ages (the slang name for a doctor or surgeon), you could probably expect to lose some blood. The procedure had a fancy name: phlebotomy. Two methods might be used, depending on your symptoms: applying blood-suckers to your body and allowing them to suck blood through your skin until they were so full they fell off, or opening a vein with a knife in the part of your body nearest to (or farthest away from) the place that hurt. You had to hope your visiting leech knew the difference between a vein and an artery (it seems some of them got it wrong!) or you'd quickly bleed to death.

Leeches—the worms, not the people—have proved useful in different ways in modern medicine. Check out the new uses for yourself. (Look in a recent encyclopedia, or search the Internet for "leech" or "leech AND medicinal.")

Monks and nuns built hospitals, cared for sick people, and sometimes performed surgery. In 1215, the Church forbade them to cut or bleed their patients, although they were allowed to treat sick and injured people in other ways. All things considered, it's possible that more patients recovered without operations than with them.

Doctors studied surgery as a subject at university, but they did not do operations. Surgeons operated, but they did not study. Strange, isn't it?

Today, physicians and surgeons belong to the same organization. They almost came together 600 years ago, when King Henry V created a joint College of Physicians and Surgeons in London. It lasted for 18 months. However, the Barbers' Guild petitioned the city, saying that barbers would not obey the law, but would practice surgery as they had in the past. The mayor gave in and dissolved the college. The surgeons of London kept their own guild for more than a hundred years, but they finally united, not with the physicians but with the barbers!

SURGEON

You perform bloodletting, operations and amputations, sometimes including battlefield surgery. Since you cannot dull your patients' pain, sometimes they die from shock. You often have to improvise and repair your own instruments, and have become expert in the necessary metalwork. You can recognize and treat some sicknesses. You are more skilled than a barber-surgeon, but, like him, you learn by apprenticeship and experience.

Perhaps your lord will go on a crusade, and you'll be lucky enough to meet an Arabian surgeon. Some ancient Egyptians, Greeks, and Romans were great surgeons, and Arabian doctors learned from their records. However, you can't read Arabic, not even the letters, and you don't do much better with Latin, so a book on surgery wouldn't help you much.

DOCTOR

It doesn't matter much if your chief ambition is to treat sick people, become rich and famous, or teach at a university: a medical career offers all these possibilities. You learn by university study, experience, reading, and contact with others, especially Islamic doctors. Your clothes are opulent and elegant, perhaps a long red gown and furred hood, with a belt of silver thread and embroidered gloves.

How do you make a diagnosis? Often, you begin with your patient's astrological chart, and examine the stars! You may consider general health and mental attitude, give advice on diet, and examine your patient's urine. Bleeding is a common treatment, though your assistant puts the bloodsuckers on the patient's body; you don't get your hands dirty.

Women practiced medicine and sometimes taught at universities, though not in England. The greatest expert in women's health and diseases was Dr. Trotula (died 1097). She taught at the University of Salerno and wrote a textbook that was used long after her death.

APOTHECARY

If you'd like to make up prescriptions, apothecary is a good career for you. You can't order what you need from a big company, though. With the help of your apprentice, you have to collect, gather, grow, or trade for everything. You have to dry your own herbs, distill your own potions, and grind seeds or minerals to powder with a pestle and mortar, and then mix salves and ointments, lotions and potions, according to your own recipes.

No government agency tests your products, so you'd better take care to get them right, especially as some of your recipes contain poisons: a little may cure, where a lot may kill.

THE BLACK DEATH

Doctors faced a horrible challenge when the plague came to Europe. It killed so many people that the population 50 years later was only half what it had been. In three ghastly years, from 1348 to 1350, millions of people died. Nobody knew how the disease was spread. Lots of people ran away from the plague, but they carried the infection with them, spreading it everywhere. Many doctors were heroes, trying to treat the sick. Of course, many doctors died.

One kind of plague infected your bloodstream. Black boils as big as an egg popped up in your armpits and groin, oozing blood and pus. You died in about five days. That variety was spread by touch. When somebody tried to feed you or bandage your sores, they caught it.

The other kind infected your lungs. You developed fever and spat blood, sweated and coughed, and died in three days or less. Sometimes a person went to bed feeling well and died before morning. That kind was spread from the breath of the sick person.

Plague came to Europe with the small black rats that lived on ships, and the fleas on those rats. A tiny bacillus moved from the rats' bloodstream to the stomach of the fleas, which then bit humans and infected them. Fleas and rats had been around for thousands of years before the Black Death. The bacillus had likely been around too, without doing much damage, but suddenly, nobody knows why, it turned deadly.

Doctors could see that infection was spread from contact with sick people, or their clothes or bodies. One famous Italian doctor thought that the poison was communicated "by air breathed out and in," but he didn't know about living things too small to see, so he decided the air must be poisoned by the influences of the planets. The medical faculty at the University of Paris also explained it by astrology: they told the king that the plague had been caused by a triple conjunction of Saturn, Jupiter, and Mars in the 40th degree of Aquarius, on March 20, 1345.

Quarantine was likely the best way to keep plague from spreading. In the Italian city of Milan, Archbishop Giovanni Visconti ordered the first three houses where plague was discovered to be walled up with everyone inside, sick, well, and dead together. Makes you shudder, doesn't it? But— Milan escaped lightly. In England, a minor nobleman burned the nearby village to keep plague from spreading to his manor house. It seems he too succeeded; his descendants still live at Noseley Hall.

HEALER; MIDWIFE

The villagers and poor folks have no money to pay for your help, but mostly they love and value you, and they give what they can. In the bitterest winter, you will not starve. Often, you know more about herbs and natural remedies than the apothecary or the doctor. Your mother was a healer before you, and hers before her. You've helped many new babies into the world; you've nursed the dying.

Often, though, the villagers' respect is mixed with fear. Year after year, Sally's babies die soon after birth. Whom does she blame? You. When the miller beats his children, he can see that you are giving him the evil eye. Sometimes it is dangerous to be a healer.

CAREGIVER FOR LEPERS

Leprosy in the Middle Ages was like HIV/AIDS today: fairly common, certain to get worse, with no known cure (though it was not spread like AIDS). The leprosy bacteria were probably spread by contact with an infected person's snot. Before the crusades, leprosy was more common in the Islamic world; it spread throughout Europe after the crusaders came home. Leprosy is an ugly disease. Starting with loss of feeling in fingers and toes, it destroys muscles and nerves, and slowly deforms the body. Most people were terrified of lepers, even though the disease is not easy to catch, even with years of exposure. Other conditions were sometimes confused with leprosy: chronic skin diseases, for example.

Many lepers were shut up in asylums, where members of religious orders devoted their lives to caring for them. Would you volunteer for this job? Perhaps you'll become one of the Knights of St. Lazarus, supervising the asylum, or one of the monks or nuns. You have no medical treatment to offer, but you keep the lepers fed, clothed and sheltered, and busy at work and prayers. It's more dangerous to help lepers who live outside the asylums, since people are afraid you've caught the disease and they'll catch it from you. You may be forced to live with the lepers yourself. Lepers are forbidden to enter inns, churches, mills, or bakehouses, to touch healthy persons or eat with them, to wash in the streams, or to walk along narrow footpaths. They have to ring a bell and shout "Unclean," so healthy people can get out of the way.

CHAPTER SIX

Sit-Down Jobs

There weren't many academic jobs in the Middle Ages, jobs where your real work was thinking rather than doing things. Some religious jobs offered a future for people with a passion for book-learning. A handful of universities became centers of learning throughout Europe. However, a sit-down job of any kind was an enormous luxury. The Middle Ages were strongly biased in favor of action. Thinking didn't qualify. Don't let that stop you from tackling the jobs in this chapter, though. You may do the world more good than 50 knights.

Europe had only one academic language in the Middle Ages: Latin. Scholars did not write in English or French or German. Because they knew Latin well, they could communicate with each other without needing translators. They could read books by authors from many different places, so long as they were in Latin. Early in the ninth century, Islamic scholars translated Euclid's great mathematical work from ancient Greek to Arabic. Unfortunately, nobody translated it from Arabic to Latin for another 300 years. Before 1000 CE, the best schools and universities were located in Arab countries and in Moorish (Arab) Spain. The medical school at Salerno, in Italy, became famous because of a doctor who had studied in Baghdad.

Oxford and Cambridge in England became centers of learning from the early 1100s. Eton, still a famous (and expensive) school for boys, was founded by King Henry VI in 1440.

SCHOOLMASTER; TEACHER

Good teachers nourish the mind and spirit. The Oxford scholar described in Chaucer's *Canterbury Tales* was eager to learn as well as to teach. However, most medieval teaching was by rote (memorization), helped by frequent whipping. Understanding was not important. "Book learning" was mostly taught by clergy, sometimes in an abbey or parsonage school, sometimes in a castle, where a priest was part of the household. As they became rich, some guilds built schools and admitted students. In the city of Florence, you would belong to one of the four following guilds, depending on what subject you taught: grammar, arithmetic, reading, or writing.

Schools were for boys; girls were taught at home. There were a few schools where bright or musically talented children, even from poor families, might find a place. Many poor scholars attended one of the universities.

A LESSON FOR TEACHERS

Coroner's Records, Oxford, 7 December 1301.

The body of John de Neushom, schoolmaster, was found by his wife Isabella and pulled out of the river. The inquest found that John had gone out after lunch in search of switches for whipping his pupils. Having climbed up a willow tree near a millpond, to cut off suitable branches, he fell in the water and drowned.

PHILOSOPHER

Most philosophers joined religious orders, where they could spend time thinking and writing. Thomas Aquinas (1225–74) studied and taught mostly at the University of Paris. He set himself to organize knowledge, to bring together ideas from ancient Greece and medieval Islam into a framework of European Christianity. He did it so well that scholars still study his work, and it remains an important basis for teaching.

Warning: Your family may not want you to be a monk-philosopher. Thomas Aquinas's mother shut him up in the family castle for a year, trying to make him change his mind.

POLYMATH

A polymath knows everything in the world! The medieval world was not as full of knowledge as ours, but even then, only a genius might come close to knowing everything. Roger Bacon (1219–94), English scientist, mathematician, and linguist, Franciscan monk and teacher at Oxford University, likely came closer than anyone else. He used his knowledge, too. He developed the idea for a paddlewheel boat, cracked Italian cipher codes, and described gunpowder (some people thought he invented it, but it was really the Chinese).

In today's Information Age, everybody is a specialist. If you want to know everything, go back to the Middle Ages.

. . . six, seven, eight . . .

ALCHEMIST

You have two goals: making lead into gold, and finding the philosopher's stone. Gold is the perfect metal; other metals want to be like gold and your job as an alchemist is to help them. The philosopher's stone is even better. It helps everything turn toward its highest form: common metals turn to gold, and human beings live for hundreds of years without getting old.

You have tried thousands of different experiments, and all of them have failed. No matter, you tell yourself, pouring a cup of melted lead into your crucible, adding a pinch of mercury and a spoonful of silver filings, blowing the bellows to make your furnace hotter, ignoring the new burns on your hands. No matter, surely this time you will succeed.

Alchemists never found what they were looking for, but sometimes they made other discoveries. Chinese alchemists found that a mixture of saltpeter, sulfur, and carbon, when heated, did not lead to immortality. It exploded and set the house on fire. They had found gunpowder.

Some alchemists were part-time confidence tricksters. If you couldn't make lead into gold, you had to get money some other way to pay for more lead bars, equipment, and chemicals. You might sneak some gold into a mixture and dupe an "investor" into thinking you had made it. If you had more equipment and materials, you could make much more gold. Even though you knew you had not made even a sprinkle of gold dust, you didn't believe it was impossible, only that you hadn't done it yet.

CLERK

You are a person who can look at strange marks on a wax tablet or a sheet of parchment and turn them into words: you can read. Monks and priests can read, so it must be part of God's plan, but ordinary people are a bit suspicious about it.

Students at the universities read all the time. Some of them will go without dinner for a month or more to buy a book. They look like beggars, all skin and bones, dressed in threadbare robes.

It was harder to read in the Middle Ages than it is today. Letters and lines were squeezed together. The same word was often spelled in several different ways. Scribes left out parts of common words to save space, but they did not always shorten the same word in the same way. The beauty of the text was sometimes more important to the copyist than clear letters.

In certain situations, reading could save your life. Most people who could read belonged to the clergy. Clerks were tried in church courts, where criminals were not executed. You might accidentally kill a person, be found guilty of manslaughter, and yet escape being hanged by "pleading your clergy." Many criminals pretended they could read. They memorized the part of the Bible that was used as the test, the first verse of Psalm 51.

ASTROLOGER

You forecast the future by observing the planets and stars and the way they come together at particular times. Astrology is an ancient science, a respectable kind of magic. Kings may ask for your advice. Yours is a prestigious career. You may use an astrolabe for locating the position of stars and planets, and algorism stones for your calculations, using another import from Islamic culture: Arabic numbers and the decimal system.

AUTHOR, NONFICTION

You write practical books: manuals on defending a castle or managing a household; "self-improvement" books, teaching good manners and behavior for noblewomen; and biographies, histories, and educational works full of advice for other people, especially younger ones.

To earn a living, you must keep writing day and night. However, if you can please your patrons, you may become a popular author like Christine de Pisan. Christine was married at age 15 and widowed at 25; she supported herself and three young children with her writing. She wrote 15 important books in six years, from 1397 to 1403, as well as smaller works, filling 70 big copybooks.

CHAPTER SEVEN

Artistic Jobs

It was not easy to make a living as an artist in the Middle Ages. (It isn't easy today, either.) Some medieval artists were monks or nuns; they lived and worked in abbeys. Others had paying jobs that allowed time for their art, or were able to sell their work for good prices. However, most artists depended on rich patrons for their living. The patron might commission a work. If it pleased him (or her), he would be especially generous with gold, precious gems, or other rewards. Even if your taste was different from his, or you longed to try something new, you had to please your patron. Nonetheless, artists brought their special vision to this age, creating works that help us to understand the hopes and ideals of people then—works that people today love and value, for their beauty and sublime qualities, or sense of fun, or unique design, or use of materials.

Medieval works are part of the heritage of humanity. Unfortunately, some people do not treat these irreplaceable items with respect. Art objects, many from the Middle Ages, were stolen from museums in Europe during the 1990s and early 2000s. The thief's mother cut up priceless canvases and wooden panels and threw millions of dollars' worth of statues, jewelry, and musical instruments into the river after her son was arrested. In Afghanistan in 2001, the governing Taliban destroyed two ancient statues of the Buddha. Some people destroy books, or anything else that does not suit them or that they cannot understand, perhaps from fear. Great art has power. Even a vandal may recognize that.

STAINED-GLASS ARTIST

You design and create huge stained-glass windows for a cathedral, made from small pieces of bright-colored glass that are put together with leaden joints. Occasionally a traveler from Venice brings glass for sale, bigger pieces than you can make, perhaps, or colors that are beyond your art. Mostly, though, you make your own glass, melting sand and silica, adding what's needed for each brilliant color. You blow the molten glass into balls, but the pieces you cut are fairly small; they look almost flat.

Sometimes you create glass jewelry, beakers, or tubing for alchemists, or clear glass windows for a rich man's home. Being cut from a ball, regular window glass is always somewhat convex, so nothing seen through it looks quite right. However, this work provides excellent training for your apprentices.

PAINTER

You create art: sometimes religious, such as Mary with baby Jesus; sometimes worldly, such as scenes of romance or hunting. You need talent, a steady hand and a good eye, self-discipline and determination, and not too much imagination, unless you're a genius— then you may make your own rules.

Your lord likes flattery. If he asks you to paint him killing a wild boar, your boar is bigger, uglier, and meaner than a real animal, and your lord becomes a great hunter, driving his spear into its throat. Your apprentices and journeymen mix the colors, prepare the media, and even paint unimportant parts of your big paintings.

The Italian genius Giotto (late 1200s and early 1300s) painted people who looked ready to move and speak, happy, sad, angry, bad-tempered, or laughing at life. He led the way toward a new kind of art in Europe.

Medieval artists used brilliant colors, but paintings before Giotto seem flat, partly because most artists did not use perspective, where faraway objects are smaller than nearby ones, and partly because the painted people don't show human feelings.

EMBROIDERER

From nobles to peasants, women decorated their clothes and homes with needlework. Full-time workers included women and men. If you were one of them, you might have learned your craft at the famous school of embroidery in Canterbury, and maybe even worked on the Bayeux Tapestry there.

One English princess's wedding clothes in 1351 included an embroidered robe of crimson velvet. You might have been one of the 20 men and 9 women who worked on it for 13 days.

BAYEUX TAPESTRY

One great work of embroidery has survived for more than 900 years: the Bayeux Tapestry. It is about half a meter (20 inches) high and more than 70 meters (230 feet) long. It tells the story of how Duke William of Normandy conquered England.

The Bayeux Tapestry includes 623 people, 202 horses, 55 dogs, and more than 500 other creatures, from birds to dragons. There are 49 trees, 41 ships, and almost 2,000 Latin words. Did I count them? No, but I looked at pictures on the Internet. So can you. Search for Bayeux Tapestry, or go to **http://www.sjolander.com/viking/museum/bt/bt.htm**

WOOD-CARVER

You carve wooden articles, from spoons to sell at the fair to statues of saints, to elaborate repeated designs for church, castle, or manor house. You and the sculptor both work in three dimensions, but you prefer wood to stone.

SCULPTOR

One of your jobs as a sculptor is to create effigies of nobles: the dead knight and lady are carved in stone, lying on top of their coffins, sometimes with their favorite dogs at their feet. Sculptors carve statues of saints for churches and cathedrals, and gargoyles with monster faces. Sometimes they carve friezes that show groups of people or tell a story.

PLAYWRIGHT

Medieval playwrights told stories from the Bible or tales of miracles. In England, groups of plays showed the whole Christian story starting with the creation of the world. In early times, these plays were performed in churches; clerics probably wrote them. For example, Abbess Hrosvitha wrote six plays about Christian virtues. (Boring.) Later plays, held outdoors, were much more fun, with plenty of comedy and practical jokes. There were 48 separate Bible story plays at one town, 24 at another. If you like to dramatize serious subjects in a fun way, be a playwright.

PLAYER (ACTOR)

Different guilds put on each play. Naturally, the shipwrights (shipbuilders) insist on doing the story of Noah, where they build the ark. Though professional actors may star, most of the players are amateurs. For them, acting is a part-time job.

The whole cycle of Bible story plays takes a few days, a good way to celebrate at Christmas or Easter. Guilds compete to put on the most elaborate or thrilling drama. The plays are staged on double-decker wagons. You perform your play, then your wagon rolls along to the next location and a new audience, and you do it again, while a different wagon moves into the place you left.

ILLUMINATOR

You decorate books, using gold and silver and brilliant colors to paint borders for each page and capital letters for each new section, as well as creating miniatures and full-page illustrations. When a rich noble hires you to make a Book of Hours, you use most of the space on each page. It doesn't matter if the scribe has to squeeze the writing. You have fun with your art, sometimes sneaking in your own face, or drawing bears with different expressions here and there.

You apprenticed with great masters, the Limbourg brothers, where you ground precious colors for one of the Duc de Berry's books: lapis lazuli for an amazing transparent ultramarine, carbonate of copper for malachite green, and arsenic trisulfide for yellow; you heated mercury and sulphur to make vermilion red. When your master gave you tips on working with these dangerous poisons, you listened!

POET; LITERARY AUTHOR

In this modern age, your parents may want you to be a doctor, a lawyer, or an accountant. Ask if they can name any doctor, lawyer, or accountant of the Middle Ages. Then ask if they have heard of Chaucer (Chaw'sir) or Dante (Don'tay). You can find books by these great poets in your public library. Chaucer was a customs officer and diplomat. Dante was born into a noble family. Both these authors experienced poverty and danger, as well as fame. However, as a medieval writer, you can't count on fame or fortune. Most poets make their living at other jobs.

In the Middle Ages, you won't find ballpoint pens, pencils, or comfortable chairs. You cut and sharpen your own quill pens, mix your own ink, and sit on a stool, hunched over a high desk. You write on vellum or parchment. It's expensive; you scrape off early drafts and reuse each piece, hoping your work will please rich patrons. When the ideas flow well, however, and the words work their magic, writing is the most splendid career in the world.

CHAPTER EIGHT
Dirty Jobs

Some medieval jobs were dirty because you had to work in filthy conditions; they were physically dirty. Other jobs were dirty because you hunted, bullied, or cheated your victims; these jobs were morally dirty. In this second kind, it was not the job that was dirty so much as the individuals doing it.

People in the Middle Ages did not wash themselves or change into clean clothes as often as we do today. If you had to carry water and heat it over an open fire, or wash in cold water outside in both winter and summer, you'd probably do the same.

Sanitation was a problem, too. There were no flush toilets. Most towns provided public latrines, but never enough of them. London, for example, had only 16 public latrines for nearly 30,000 people. Many city homes had private cesspits, sometimes in the backyard, sometimes underneath the floorboards inside the house, lined with bricks or wicker. When the smell grew unbearable, you called in the gong farmer. Toilets in a castle might be little rooms jutting out from an outside wall, with a hole in the floor. Sometimes a river ran underneath and carried away the waste. Otherwise, urine and bowel movements fell into a ditch. Workers cleared the ditch.

Some medieval sanitation systems were excellent, though. Abbeys and castles often had a separate latrine building. Some castles had latrines on every floor; these drained into covered stone ditches with ventilating holes and openings for waste removal, or into underground pits. Archeologists studying the ruins of old castles sometimes mistook a stone-covered sewer for a secret passage, or a cesspit for a dungeon!

Peasants' clothing of rough wool did not wash well, nor did nobles' costumes of velvet embroidered with jewels and trimmed with fur. A few rich people bathed often, and even took a metal bathtub along when traveling, as well as servants to heat the water, but this was rare. Dirt came with most jobs: the peasant grubbing in the field, the blacksmith at his forge, the alchemist at his furnace, or the knight sweating in his armor, smelling strongly of horse. Women were no cleaner than men. The rushes on the floor of the great hall at the castle were usually replaced only twice a year: fall and spring. Meat bones and food scraps, dog hair and other debris fell and were hidden, not to be swept out until months later. However, some jobs were outstandingly filthy—these are the physically dirty ones you'll find in this chapter.

STREET CLEANER

Cities made laws against emptying chamber pots in the streets. However, if nobody saw you, you'd get away with it. If you worked for a rich or noble family, you'd get away with it too. Horses, pigs, and other animals did what they were going to do anyway. There were no sidewalks. There were never enough street cleaners, even when the weather was dry. When it was wet, manure and mud soiled your feet. Shoes with high platform soles were sometimes fashionable, or pattens strapped to your shoes to lift your feet above the stinking mud. Rich folk held pomanders (spice balls) to their noses when they went into the street.

The latrine attendant had a more disgusting job than that of the street cleaner—but not all that much more disgusting.

GONG FARMER

GONG FARMER (LATRINE ATTENDANT)

As careers go, this was a stinker—and so was that pun. A latrine or privy (gong) was the toilet of the Middle Ages. As a gong "farmer," you dig out cesspits and sort through the excrement for your harvest. You wash and then sell or use everything you find, like a silver penny, a glove, or a button. (Yuck.) You throw the sewage into a river or spread it on vegetable gardens as manure. (Double yuck.)

Some people believed that attendants at public latrines were immune to the plague, a bonus if it had been true. Did they think the horrible smell would drive death away? It didn't.

BATHHOUSE ATTENDANT

Public bathhouses were popular in towns throughout Europe. Hot springs were centers for therapy. Baths were open all day except on Sundays and holidays.

As an attendant, you carry hot water for the wooden tubs or for the steam rooms. You soap and massage your customers, shampoo their hair, and offer extras such as manicures or deodorants. What with insults and splashing, yours is a rough job, and you get dirtier as the day goes on. Clients share the tubs. You add hot water now and then, but you don't clean out your tubs until you have to. This is a steamy job, as well as a dirty one. You wear a light tunic with shoulder straps, and a hairnet so that your clients can't grab your hair and pull you in.

MEDIEVAL COSMETICS

Bathhouse attendants might prepare and sell any of these:
- hand lotion: asphodel—a plant from the lily family—and egg white
- mouthwash: honey, cucumbers, and water
- hair perfume: musk
- deodorant (for stinking armpits): strawberry and herbs

MINER

During a siege, you tunnel toward the enemy's castle and dig out a big space underneath part of the wall. An engineer plots your route. You support the underground room with posts soaked in tallow and fill it with dry wood, grease—anything that burns well—setting it on fire as you leave. The posts burn, the earth caves in and the wall crumbles. With luck (and an engineer who gets his calculations right), the castle's defenders won't know anything until they see the smoke.

Your job may also be to mine mineral ore, coal, or salt. Medieval England produced tin, lead, silver, gold, iron, and other metals, mostly from open pits, but later from underground. Gold miners were often paid with ore. Women and children, as well as men, worked as miners. Toward the end of the Middle Ages, water-powered machinery was used for pumping out mine workings.

PARDONER

"Pardoner" is a church job of a kind. If you are a pardoner, you are a cheat. You sell fake pardons from God for sins—even sins as serious as murder. Wielding a few words of Latin and a parchment scroll, you promise your customers that God has forgiven their evil deeds. Sometimes you sell a pardon even before a villain has committed a crime. You also peddle fake holy relics, such as the bones of a saint (really pigs' bones), pieces of the cross on which Jesus was crucified (slivers of any old wood), or a piece of the sail from St. Peter's fishing boat (a scrap of sailcloth from some old boat).

Your victims are usually poor and ignorant. Supposing someone made a vow to go to church every day for a year if her child recovered from smallpox. Her child recovered, but every day the walk to church seems longer. Winter comes. How can she get out of a promise to God? As the pardoner, you will fix it for her—and take her hen in payment. Many clergy believe you are worse than a murderer. A murderer kills a person's body; a pardoner's victims might lose their souls!

WITCH HUNTER

Was a witch hunter a representative of law and order, whose work was necessary to keep people's souls safe from the devil? Or was he an evil person, and this one of the dirtiest of jobs?

If you accuse a village woman of witchcraft out of jealousy and a desire to take her property, this is clearly dirty work. If she dies on the ducking stool, you deserve to have nightmares. (A ducking stool was a chair on the end of a long plank. The accused person was tied to the chair and ducked repeatedly in a river or lake.) However, if you are convinced that she really is a follower of Satan, and therefore a danger to the soul of every man and woman in the village, you will feel that the sooner the danger is removed, the better. Is your accusation still dirty work?

Most people in the Middle Ages believed that some people, men as well as women, were witches. King James I of England wrote a book called *Daemonology*, about witches and his experiences with them. If the village crone wished a pox on the boy who threw stones at her and he died soon afterward, his family might accuse her of causing his death. A mentally disabled person might speak strangely; an epileptic might have a seizure. Any strange behavior might seem like witchcraft to ignorant and superstitious people (clergy and other educated people as well as villagers). If they found a witchy creature in a suspect's home, such as a toad or a black cat, they felt sure they had found a witch.

Sometimes it was an advantage if people thought you were a witch. They paid you to curse their enemies or to make love potions. However, you lived in danger. Thousands of people accused of being witches were put to death.

CHAPTER NINE

Law and Order Jobs

People often complain today that laws have become too complicated. If laws were simpler, they say, we wouldn't need so many lawyers. You might think the legal system was simpler in the Middle Ages. Many arguments were settled in battle, and many lords kept order by force and cruel punishments. Films and television programs set in the Middle Ages show plenty of fights, but very few law-court scenes.

Medieval legal systems, however, were not simpler than ours. To start with, there were two systems, each quite different from the other: canon law (Church law, which included family law) and common law. There were dozens of different kinds of courts, and hundreds of different people entitled to make laws, rules, or regulations, and to enforce them. Everybody had a part in keeping order in the land. Even the peasants had to raise the "hue and cry" if they saw a criminal act or observed a felon escaping. This meant using horns to make a noise, and yelling as well, while you chased the villain. You were not allowed to be a bystander. If a villager hid a criminal, the whole village could be fined.

> ... in the feast of Saint George last year at Bedford a horse of William Exton, price of fifteen shillings feloniously he should have stolen the which indictment was to him purposed maliciously, he thereof not being guilty, as all the country knoweth, considering that he was at the time that the said felony was supposed and long before at London ...

In England, some laws and courts grew out of Anglo-Saxon ways. Some arrived with the Norman French, some came from the Church, and some—especially those relating to ships and the sea, and to trade with foreigners—were based on the ancient Roman law of the sea. What a mixture! How on earth did it work?

Actually, it probably worked about as well as our legal system does today: sometimes well enough, sometimes badly. Records are spotty. There were no court reporters. Apprentice lawyers made summaries of some cases, but they were only interested in the arguments, not the outcome of a trial, so we often don't know who won. In a general way, church courts were more humane; kings' courts were more insistent on the letter of the law.

LAWYER

Tie your new white silk coif under your chin! Today, you are to plead your very first case in court. You have memorized the arguments, and indeed the words. If you forget a word or two, the case will be thrown out, your client will lose his land—and you certainly won't be paid. Luckily, your master has taught you well, and you have sat in court day after day, watching other experts and making notes of their arguments. When this court traveled on its circuit of towns and villages, you went as your master's clerk. Some day surely you will be a serjeant-at-law, and practice in the Court of Common Pleas, helping to make common law for the whole country.

Your cousin Robert is a newly-made Doctor of Laws from Oxford University and lords it over you like a great man. Oxford does not give courses in common law, nor does Cambridge. You have to study in the Inns of Court in London, and make your reputation on the job. However, you're not jealous of your cousin. Robert studied Church law; he argues in the Bishop's Court. Lately, he pleaded the case of Mistress Alice, who said she had married Alan of Stavely and wanted her rights as his wife. Alan did not deny the claim, but he said he was only 11 years old at the time, not 12, the legal age. He didn't like Alice and had never lived with her. Cousin Robert (and Alice) won, though; the court decided it was a legal marriage.

PROVOST

A poor noble may do this job for a great lord. In towns, guild leaders hire provosts. On a noble estate, you settle disputes among peasants and deal out justice in minor matters, putting guilty people in the stocks or even hanging them. In town, you investigate offenses against guild rules; for example, a weaver who stiffens cheap fabric and sells it for the price of high-quality material. You have the power to seize all his fabric and burn it, and to destroy his looms. He will be ruined.

SUMMONER

I hereby summon thee to court on a charge of theft.

SUMMONER (in a common-law court) or BEADLE (in a Church court)

You are a petty officer of a court of law. When an ordinary person is charged with an offense or called as a witness, you must find the person, explain the charge, and warn him or her to appear in court. You also usher litigants and witnesses into court.

HEADSMAN; HANGMAN

Once convicted of a serious crime, noble people were usually beheaded; common people were usually hanged. Either way, a condemned person was just as dead.

As a royal headsman (tops in this career), you expect to do your job with one well-placed stroke of ax or sword. Even if you don't enjoy your work, you are proud of your skill. You always ask the victim to forgive you; he or she usually does. You get the person's clothes, which may be valuable, so you try not to get too much blood on them.

For every noble condemned to death, there are dozens of peasants, so as a hangman you'll get plenty of practice. If you are good at your job, you can arrange to break your victim's neck, giving a quick death, or you can let the condemned person strangle slowly and painfully. People try not to offend you.

TORTURER

Torture was a nasty fact of life in the Middle Ages, just as it is a nasty fact of life in some countries today, but there was no Amnesty International then to oppose it. Torture was the usual way of getting a confession to a crime, after which the victim might not object too much to being hanged. Some medieval careers make any more or less normal modern person feel sick.

It is your job to cause physical pain, usually in order to force somebody to say or do something. How can anybody do this? Perhaps you can look at human beings as objects, not as people, even when they bleed and scream. Perhaps you can believe that information or a confession will be useful to the people you serve, or even to the victim. Perhaps you are a sadist, a sick person who likes to inflict pain. Perhaps nobody who reads this book wants to do this job—let's hope so.

MEDIEVAL VIEWS ABOUT TORTURE

The Church might hand people over to be tortured if things they said or did were contrary to the Church's teachings. It was believed it didn't matter if people suffered on earth provided that their souls were saved.

A noble who wanted somebody's property might arrest and torture the person until he confessed to some crime. Then the person could be hanged and his property seized. In time of war, both sides tortured anybody who might be a spy. Brigands tortured (or threatened to torture) their captives in case they were hiding money or jewels. Most villages had their stocks, where petty offenders were locked up while others shouted insults and pelted them with garbage, a sport enjoyed by many.

People today need not be too smug. Most readers can think of some modern sports where one person tries to hurt another while spectators cheer.

MONEY CHANGER

Different currencies were common in the Middle Ages, since traders brought coins from many parts of the world. Money changers were much in demand at big fairs, where foreign merchants brought goods to sell. There was no paper money. Coins were worth the value of the metal in them.

As a money changer, you must know the value of different coins, so that you can trade foreign coins for familiar ones, wherever you happen to be. It's tricky. Sometimes gold or silver has been cut from a coin, so it weighs less than it should; sometimes lead has been mixed with the precious metal. You use a balance (a kind of scale) to weigh the coins, and can often detect short weight or impurity by weighing a customer's coin against one of your own. You travel with merchants, making the rounds of the fairs. Nobles may try to borrow money from you, but it's hard to get them to pay it back.

SHERIFF

Your job is to govern a shire (the "Shire Reeve"); you are governor, judge, and coroner combined. Many people don't like you, because you collect the king's taxes. You don't decide the amount—the king does that—but when the winter food supply has gone for taxes and people are starving, they blame you. You're busy enforcing laws, summoning jurors, catching criminals, maintaining royal castles, keeping merchants in line, executing royal writs and decrees, holding inquests, and presiding over four different courts, not to mention seizing persons, lands, and goods; supervising elections; repairing public buildings; and keeping records.

I'm warning you Goodwife Baxter. If I catch you selling stale bread again it's a day in the stocks for you.

Kings liked to believe that God was on their side. Bandit companies didn't care. Good pay, good arms, good food, and good leaders mattered to them. They could always repent their sins later and be forgiven, like the wicked Frenchman Arnaut de Cervole. The pope paid a fortune of 40,000 écus and pardoned Cervole and all his company so that the bandits would leave him alone (protection money!).

Sir Robert Knollys was an English brigand leader. After a long and bloody career in France and Italy, he gave up being a brigand and rejoined the English king. He kept his money. The king gave him land and arranged a good marriage. Knollys became a powerful noble and good family man and died in his bed.

For someone without much conscience, brigand could be a rewarding career.

BANDIT

BANDIT or BRIGAND (OUTLAW)

Brigands formed armies in Italy and France in the late Middle Ages. Exiles, outlaws, bankrupt and landless knights, and adventurers from all over Europe joined together and fought for pay. Leading one of these armies could make a man rich and powerful.

Most future brigands had left home to follow their lords into war. When fighting stopped for the winter, they had no way to get home. Often, they had not been paid. They were already used to seizing grain and animals for food. When they became brigands, nothing much changed, except that now they could choose their leaders and they were paid on time, with bonuses.

In the regular army, most generals were promoted because of their influential families; they didn't have to know anything about armies and warfare. Many nobles only cared about how they looked on the field of battle, like a sports player who wants to be a star and doesn't care about the team. Brigand companies chose their own generals, leaders who were tough and ruthless, who would win money and loot without losing men.

Outlaws were men "outside the law." When a man was outlawed, the king received all his property. Until 1329, anybody could kill an outlaw without penalty.

ENFORCER OF LAWS AGAINST RICH CLOTHES

Nobles were angry when a doctor looked like a duke, or a merchant's wife dressed like a lady. They passed laws—called sumptuary laws—about who could wear silks and velvets, expensive colors, fur trim and jewels, or extreme fashions, like shoes with long, pointed toes that had to be tied to your knee so that you would not trip. They hired officials to enforce these laws.

If you are hired, your job will be to find women and men who are not noble, but who wear rich clothes and travel around in big, fancy carriages, and charge them with breaking the law. In the Italian city of Florence, you can chase after merchants' wives in the street and enter their houses to search closets and trunks. You don't need a warrant. If you like silks and velvets and jewelled embroidery, you'll see plenty in this job.

In one merchant's house in Florence, officers seized cloth of white marbled silk embroidered with vine leaves and red grapes, a coat with white and red roses on a pale yellow ground, and another coat of blue cloth decorated with white lilies and red stars and compasses, lined with red-striped cloth. Rich people had some amazing clothes.

In France, rich lords and ladies could order four new outfits each year; poorer knights and ladies could have three. Boys and girls could order only one new outfit each year. In England, a merchant worth £1,000 could wear the same clothes as a knight worth £500, and a merchant worth £200 the same clothes as a knight worth £100. Being twice as rich was as good as being noble! Peasants could not wear any color except black or brown. All of these laws were often disobeyed.

Who do you think you are, wearing a hood of vermilion?!

CHAPTER TEN

Traveling Jobs

Most people in the Middle Ages never went more than a few miles from the place where they were born. Men sometimes had to leave their fields to fight, but they usually did not go far, and the fighting was usually not prolonged.

Many people did travel, however—some only once in a lifetime, perhaps on a crusade, but others constantly, on the job. These careers, and the careers that depended on them, are described in this chapter. There were no motels in medieval times, but if there had been no travelers, there would have been no inns.

How did people communicate with others at a distance when there were no phones and no mail delivery? They traveled to visit each other or sent messages, often memorized, though sometimes in writing. How did they hear about great events? A storyteller arrived with songs and long poems, old and new. The traveler often exaggerated a tale to make it more exciting, or maybe forgot one part and made something up, and then the next person to tell the story changed it again. It's not always easy for a modern historian to find out if a thousand knights really fought in a battle, or only a hundred!

People traveled for many reasons: business, diplomacy, pilgrimage, carriage of goods by land or sea, messages, study, consultation, war, and curiosity.

MESSENGER

The king of England traveled with 12 messengers. They were paid three pence a day on the road, plus money for shoes. The king of France employed up to 100 messengers.

Lord Ronald has only one messenger: you. Your job today is to carry orders to his bailiff, 160 kilometers (100 miles) away. You should arrive in two days if your horse doesn't throw a shoe. Spring rain has made the roads muddy, but better mud than dust; you don't expect hail, sleet, or snow. Spring weather makes robbers bolder, though, so you won't wear your lord's livery. You'll dress like a poor yeoman and hope no outlaws appear. Lord Ronald's message is long and complicated, but your memory has never failed. If you had to, you could ride day and night.

MINSTREL; JONGLEUR

Minstrels and jongleurs are the rock stars of the Middle Ages. In addition to being a songwriter and singer, you have to accompany yourself, probably on the lute. Storytelling skills are important; so are acrobatic stunts, for times when the audience is bored with songs.

You may live and work in a noble household, or you may walk from town to town, playing on the street like a busker today. You'll be a welcome guest at manor or castle when you perform great poems of war, like the *Song of Roland*, or romantic legends of ancient Greece or King Arthur's court. A noble may hire you to perform songs he has written.

TROUBADOUR

You write lyrics and music and perform at court, accompanying yourself on the lute. You are the upscale version of the jongleur, but you don't do stunts. As befits a member of the nobility, you keep your dignity.

From time to time, you compete with other troubadours in "tournaments of song." Rather than singing yourself, you may hire minstrels to perform your songs of love, chivalry, religion, politics, or war, or your long song-stories about great heroes.

HOW THE TROUBADOUR SAVED THE KING (1193)

Richard the Lionhearted, king of England, was imprisoned for years somewhere in Europe. Blondel the troubadour traveled from castle to castle, singing his songs and trying to hear even a rumor that would lead to his beloved king. At last he came by chance to the right place, a castle in Austria.

From the tiny window of his cell, the king saw Blondel walking in the garden below. How could he send a message to his friend without letting his enemies know? The king sang the first lines of a song that he and Blondel had composed together; Blondel sang the rest, then took his news to the king's friends. Now they could ransom him.

TOWN CRIER

Town criers carried news and made announcements. Paris had six master criers appointed by the city. King William sent out criers after he conquered England in 1066.

As a crier in London, you wear splendid red and gold robes, white breeches, black boots, and a tricorn hat with plumes of white ostrich feathers. Like the mail carrier today, you have your route. You "cry" your message at one street corner, then move on to the next, ringing your hand bell. Sometimes you advertise special events. Everybody stops work when they hear your bell and your "Oyez, oyez." What news will you have today?

INNKEEPER

The best-known innkeeper of the Middle Ages was a fine fellow, the host of the Tabard Inn. However, he is a character in a famous poem, not a real person. Most real innkeepers of the time run sleazy operations. If you are one of them, you promise delicious food and beds piled high with feather comforters, but when your guests have paid, they get thin stew and straw mattresses full of bedbugs and lice—and they'll be lucky if you don't rob them or send word to outlaws who can rob them after they leave.

Three or four travelers—or more—often have to share one bed. (They say that 50 people can sleep in the Great Bed of Ware!) Merchants carry their own food and bedding and bring their own armed guards. To be fair, some innkeepers give good value. If you had a busier location, on a main pilgrimage road, you could afford to do that too.

Oyez, oyez! Robert Hood seen in forest with gang of jolly men, stealing from rich, giving to poor. You've been warned!

Welcome to my Inn, weary travelers

PILGRIM

You are the tourist of the Middle Ages, traveling to a place that's important in your religion. For safety on the road, you join a large group. Perhaps you are a penitent, on pilgrimage because you have done something wicked and want to be forgiven; perhaps you are disabled and hope for a miracle cure, or you're thankful because you've come safe home from war. You don't need any special reason, though.

In England, Canterbury is the most popular pilgrimage destination. Here Archbishop Thomas à Becket was murdered at the altar of his own cathedral. The king was blamed, and the pope commanded him to show how sorry he was by making his pilgrimage bare-foot, wearing itchy sackcloth, while monks beat him with knotted whips.

You have dreamed of making a pilgrimage to the Holy Land (Jerusalem), but the long journey might take the rest of your life. Who knows if you would ever return?

GEOFFREY CHAUCER AND *THE CANTERBURY TALES*

Geoffrey Chaucer wrote an extraordinary poem about a pilgrimage. In the poem, pilgrims gather at the Tabard Inn, near London, for their trip to Canterbury. They're a mixed lot: minor nobles, religious women and men, townspeople, country folk, and a sailor; high status—a knight—to low—a plowman. (The plowman is a peasant; his brother, the parish priest, is treating him to the trip.)

Chaucer paints a word picture of them all: the prioress; the university student; the business-woman from Bath who boasts that she's been married five times; the jolly friar; the miller; the summoner and the pardoner, two rogues who ride together—31 pilgrims altogether, including the innkeeper and the poet himself. For entertainment along the way, they agree that each pilgrim will tell a story. Chaucer wrote the stories they might have told. You'd find it difficult to read his poem the way he wrote it, in Middle English, but modern English versions are easy. Because a great poet wrote in so much detail about these pilgrims, *The Canterbury Tales* is the best original source of information about how ordinary people lived at the time.

CARTER (CARRIER)

You are the trucker of the Middle Ages, but your horsepower comes from horses or oxen, not from a gasoline engine. With the new kind of harness, four or six or even eight animals can be harnessed to your cart, so you can move heavier loads than your father with his single horse. Your job is moving blocks of stone from the quarry to the new cathedral. They call it "new," though your grandfather hauled stone for it, as well as your father. There will be work here for your son.

When the merchants come for the fair, you talk to the carters who carry their goods: broadcloth from Flanders, or precious cinnamon and pepper and other spices, too expensive for you to buy. They travel to far places, always on the move. Their carts are lighter than yours, and the wheels don't get caught so often in the mud when it rains. Even though peasants sometimes pilfer cobblestones, and potholes abound, the old Roman roads are still better than the muddy tracks, though nobody could drive a chariot on them anymore. Another carter comes through town every

Tuesday. He carries cloth to London and takes sugar and spices back to Worcestershire.

You drove the lady of the manor once, when she couldn't sit astride her horse and had to ride in a litter, a ramshackle kind of cart. Poor lady, she had a jolting!

TRAVELING MERCHANT

TRAVELING MERCHANT; SPECIALTY MERCHANT

Your grandparents were peddlers who went from village to village selling their pots and ribbons and rough cloth. Sometimes they set up their booth at a fair and stayed for a week or two. In winter, they moved back to town to make and buy new stock. Your father expanded, selling salt and spices. He traveled to Europe for broadcloth and lace, and once to Italy for silk and glass.

From early spring until snowfall, your family moved from one fair to the next. You grew up with the business. This is lucky, because your business isn't as simple as it used to be. Most towns now have their own market square, and the town merchants often sell the same stock as you, at much the same price. How can you compete? You decide to limit what you buy and sell, and go for quantity. If you buy a shipload of broadcloth and lace, you'll get a better price; then you can sell to merchants in town for sale to their customers. Everybody can make a living.

IMPORTER; EXPORTER

You buy up whatever your country has plenty of, fill your ships, sail where your cargo is scarce, and sell it. Then you buy whatever is cheaper there than at home, sail back, and sell the new cargo. Then you begin again. If you know what you're doing, you should make money every time. Of course, you have expenses: ships to buy or build, warehouses, carts that move cargo on land. Other people work for you, and you must make sure they don't cheat. That's not the only risk. A ship may sink or be captured.

Ships are often gone for months, even for years, and you don't know if they will ever come back. Sometimes you have to borrow money from a moneylender. You love this job, though, from the dirty coal and iron you export from Plymouth, to the wine and olives, spices, silks, and delicate glass you bring back home, sometimes by way of Venice from Persia, where camel trains bring goods from the end of the world—China.

EXPLORER

Do you want to boldly go where no one has gone before? In the Middle Ages, the world was full of places Europeans had forgotten or had never visited. If you want to be remembered, though, you must write everything down. Norse voyagers like Leif Erikson were fearless adventurers and great sailors, but they left no written records. Marco Polo the Venetian (1254–1324) is the most famous European explorer of the Middle Ages, because of his book. He served the Khan in China, who sent him to govern cities, seaports, and distant provinces, and to write detailed reports. Marco Polo belonged to a merchant family; he went to China with his uncle and cousin, who were not writers.

The greatest explorer in the Muslim world was Ibn Batuta (1304?–1368?). He traveled a greater distance and visited more parts of the world than any other explorer of the Middle Ages, including Marco Polo; and he dictated a book. Foreign rulers valued him too. For eight years, he worked for the sultan of Delhi; later, the Mongol emperor sent him as ambassador to China. Ibn Batuta's family were judges, not merchants, but he gave up the study of law at age 21, when he made his pilgrimage to Mecca and the travel bug bit him.

RECOMMENDED FURTHER READING

Here are some wonderful books of fiction to give you more of the big picture of medieval times:

Bradford, Karleen. The Crusades Trilogy: *There Will Be Wolves*, 1992.

The daughter of an apothecary, Ursula wants to become a great healer, but her ambition makes her an outsider. When she is accused of witchcraft and sentenced to burn at the stake, she is given one chance to save herself: she must join the People's Crusade to Jerusalem.

Shadows on a Sword, 1996. The young knight Theo eagerly embarks on the First Crusade.

Lionheart's Scribe, 1999. Matthew's quick wits save a queen from imprisonment and a young Muslim girl from drowning at sea. And King Richard himself soon needs a scribe.

Cushman, Karen. *Catherine, Called Birdy*. Newbery Honor 1995.

"Dear Diary, 20th Day of March, 1291.

Shaggy Beard wishes to take me to wife! What a monstrous joke… Corpus bones, I must make a plan. Luckily I am experienced at outwitting suitors."

Cushman, Karen. *The Midwife's Apprentice*. Newbery Medal 1996.

This novel is about a homeless, nameless waif who gets the village midwife to take her in, put her to work, and teach her.

de Angeli, Marguerite. *The Door in the Wall*. Newbery Medal 1950.

This classic is the story of Robin, crippled son of a mighty lord. He survives the plague deaths of his family, proves his courage, and earns recognition from the king.

Park, Linda Sue. *A Single Shard*. Newbery Medal 2002.

Set in 12th century Korea, this is the story of Tree-ear who lives under a bridge with his disabled older friend, Crane-man. Tree-ear becomes fascinated with the potter's craft and longs to create celadon ceramics. However, pottery is a trade passed on from father to son and Tree-ear is an orphan.

Scott, Walter, Sir. *Ivanhoe*, 1820.

Set in England soon after Richard Lionheart returned from the Third Crusade, and first published almost 200 years ago, *Ivanhoe*'s themes are current today: sisterhood of Jewess and English princess, Robin Hood's ideas of justice, and the hero's attempts to reconcile Saxons and Normans. The chief villain is a Templar, one of the fighting monks, who behaves in a distinctly unmonklike fashion.

Scott's novel *The Talisman* is a tale of the crusades that shows both Christian and Muslim leaders as noble human beings.

Don't expect modern political correctness or writing style. These novels are not easy, but Scott was a great storyteller, and the persevering reader will be rewarded.

ACKNOWLEDGMENTS

This book owes a debt to many authors and much research, past and present, but even more to the people who made records, and their successors and descendants who kept those records safe and gave others access to them: the clerks who recorded coroners' inquests; the bailiffs who kept lists of rents and payments; the parish priests who maintained registries of baptism, marriage, and death; the engineers, artisans, and artists who made drawings (and buildings); the lawyers who drew agreements, conveyances, and wills; and all the multitude of government and guild officials who did their bureaucratic duties; the women and men who treasured clothing and tapestries, plows, and looms. From legal documents to letters to shopping lists, even the most casual surviving record or artifact may help us to understand how people lived and worked so long ago. Authors and artists have helped too, none more so than the poet Geoffrey Chaucer with his pilgrims of *The Canterbury Tales*.

The Internet has made a growing number of original documents and scholarly commentaries available. I've also done research in libraries, including my personal library. As a teenager, I loved Prof. William Sterns Davis's *Life on a Mediaeval Barony* (1923); my parents' copy now graces my shelves. Davis illuminates the 13th century; Barbara Tuchmann's splendid *A Distant Mirror* focuses on the 14th. Much recent research has explored the position and work of women: for example, Madeleine Pelner Cosman's *Women at Work in Medieval Europe* (2000) and Judith Bennett's *Ale, Beer, and Brewsters in England: Women's work in a changing world, 1300-1600* (1996).

People have helped too. It seems to me both appropriate and typical of our multicultural society that editors, designer, and author include folks with Jewish and Protestant heritage, that Catholics have given expert advice (including a consultation with a visiting Dean of Canon Law from Rome), and that the manuscript has been read with care by teachers whose students bring ethnic and religious backgrounds from all over the world. To name a few, I thank Dr. Ron Thomson, Director of Publications at the Pontifical Institute of Mediaeval Studies, University of Toronto, editor Barbara Pulling, designer Sheryl Shapiro, and illustrator Martha Newbigging who has done an amazing job. It's been good fun working with her. I also thank the members of my writing group who have encouraged me through three years of drafts and rewrites.

It's been a challenge. The Middle Ages were very different from our time, and different from place to place and generation to generation; and there are many gaps in our knowledge and understanding. Experts don't always agree, and a book for young readers inevitably simplifies and condenses what is known. My objective has been to offer a lure that is entertaining as well as instructive, an entrée to a time that's more fascinating, not less so, when the romantic trappings of television and film are set aside.

Index